T0129471

Cross Creek Cookery

by

Marjorie Kinnan Rawlings

with drawings by
Robert Camp

A FIRESIDE BOOK
Published by Simon & Schuster
New York • London • Toronto • Sydney

FIRESIDE
Rockefeller Center
1230 Avenue of the Americas
New York, NY 10020

First Fireside Edition 1996

FIRESIDE and colophon are registered trademarks
of Simon & Schuster Inc.

Manufactured in the United States of America

7   9   10   8

Library of Congress Cataloging-in-Publication Data
Rawlings, Marjorie Kinnan.
Cross Creek cookery / by Marjorie Kinnan Rawlings ;
with drawings by Robert Camp.
p.   cm.
"A Fireside book."
Reprint. Originally published: New York :
C. Scribner's Sons, 1942.
Includes index.
1. Cookery, American.   I. Title.
TX715.R26   1996
641.5975—dc20   95-47825
CIP
ISBN 0-684-81878-7

Cross Creek Cookery

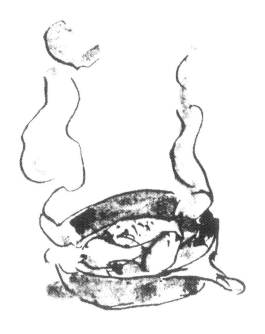

Contents

Luncheon Dishes or, The Embroidery Club

Vegetables

Potatoes, Rice, and Grits

Florida Sea Foods

Game and Meats

Salads

Desserts

Preserves, Jellies and Marmalades

Cross Creek Menus

Recipes are given for dishes marked *

BREAKFAST

Orange Juice
Creamed Sweetbreads
* Waffles *(see page 36)*
Choice of Florida Honey, Maple Syrup, Cane Syrup
    and Guava Jelly
Strong Coffee
Dora's Cream

Grapefruit
Alachua County Country Sausage
* Sour Cream Muffins *(see page 35)*
* Wild Orange Marmalade *(see page 208)*
Strong Coffee
Dora's Cream

Orange Cup
Scrambled Eggs
Bacon   Hot Biscuits
* Cheese Grits *(see page 73)*
Blackberry Jelly
Strong Coffee
Dora's Cream

Grapefruit Juice
* Sautéed Lamb's Kidneys with Sherry Gravy *(see page 112)*

TOAST
WILD GRAPE JELLY
STRONG COFFEE
DORA'S CREAM

ORANGE JUICE
VERY SMALL CRISP-FRIED ORANGE LAKE BREAM
★ GRITS (*see page* 72)
★ CORNMEAL MUFFINS (*see page* 25)
★ KUMQUAT MARMALADE (*see page* 211)
STRONG COFFEE
DORA'S CREAM

LUNCHEON

BEVERAGES TO TASTE

★ IDELLA'S CHEESE SOUFFLÉ (*see page* 44)
★ CARROTS GLAZED IN HONEY (*see page* 53)
★ HOT BISCUITS (*see pages* 20–22)
★ MAYHAW JELLY (*see page* 212)
GREEN SALAD MIXED
★ PEACH SHORT-CAKE (*see page* 183)

CREAMED CHICKEN
WAFFLES
GRAPEFRUIT AND KUMQUAT SALAD, FRENCH DRESSING
★ STRAWBERRY CHIFFON PIE (*see page* 178)

★ JELLIED CHICKEN (*see page* 41)
CREAMED NEW POTATOES

★ BEET AND CABBAGE SALAD, BOILED DRESSING (*see page* 146)
HOT BISCUITS
CAFÉ PARFAIT

★ CRAB À LA NEWBURG, CROSS CREEK (*see page* 83)
TOAST POINTS
SAUTERNE OR CHABLIS OR WHITE RHINE WINE
TOSSED SALAD OF ENDIVE, THINLY SLICED RADISHES AND
    CUCUMBERS, TART FRENCH DRESSING

★ COLLARD GREENS WITH WHITE BACON (*see page* 57)
★ CORNBREAD (*see page* 25)
SPRING ONIONS
THIS IS A MEAL

★ DEEP-FRIED ST. AUGUSTINE SHRIMP (*see page* 87)
TARTAR SAUCE
POTATO CHIPS
TOASTED BUTTERED CRACKERS
COMBINATION SALAD—TOMATOES, CUCUMBERS, RADISHES,
    GREEN PEPPERS, ONIONS
ALE OR BEER IF DESIRED
NO DESSERT, EVER

★ ORANGE LAKE FROG-LEGS, FRIED IN DORA'S BUTTER (*see page* 99)
★ STUFFED POTATOES (*see page* 66)
★ CROSS CREEK BROCCOLI À LA HOLLANDAISE (*see page* 50)
CELERY, OLIVES, RADISHES
★ CORNMEAL MUFFINS (*see page* 25)
★ MOTHER'S ORANGE PUDDING (*see page* 168)

★ EGG CROQUETTES (see page 40)
BRUSSELS SPROUTS, LEMON BUTTER
HOT BISCUITS
MAYHAW JELLY
★ TOMATO ASPIC AND ARTICHOKE SALAD,
      MAYONNAISE (see page 139)
★ ORANGE CHIFFON PIE (see page 176)

★ CREAMED POKE-WEED ON TOAST (see page 57)
CRISP BREAKFAST BACON
★ WILD GRAPE JELLY (see page 214)

★ SLICED COLD BAKED PEANUT-FED HAM (see page 114)
★ CHAYOTES AU GRATIN (see page 56)
MUFFINS
TOMATO STUFFED WITH COTTAGE CHEESE, DICED
      CUCUMBER, MINCED ONION AND GREEN PEPPER

★ PECAN PATTIES (see page 47)
★ SWEET POTATOES IN ORANGE BASKETS (see page 76)
FRESH ASPARAGUS SALAD, FRENCH DRESSING
MELBA TOAST
★ ORANGE GELATINE (see page 186)

★ GREEN PEPPERS STUFFED WITH MINCED LAMB (see page 134)
★ CHINESE CABBAGE COOKED WITH MINCED ONION
      AND BACON (see page 63)
CORN MUFFINS
GUAVA JELLY, CREAM CHEESE, CRACKERS

★ Swamp Cabbage (Hearts of Palm) Cooked with
     White Bacon or with Cream and Butter (*see page* 65)
★ Cornbread (*see page* 25)
★ Wild Orange Marmalade (*see page* 207)
★ Black Bottom Pie (*see page* 173)

DINNER

★ Baked Sherried Grapefruit (*see page* 195)
★ Squab-size Roast Chickens Stuffed with Buttered
     Crumbs and Pecans, Sherry Basting (*see page* 106)
   Giblet Gravy
★ Fluffy Rice (*see page* 74)
   Hot Biscuits
   Whole Cauliflower, Surrounded by Whole Carrots
     Arranged Like the Spokes of a Wheel, Melted
     Butter
   Romaine and Water Cress Salad, French Dressing
★ Baba au Rhum (*see page* 172)

★ Greek Lemon Soup (*see page* 10)
★ Blackbibd Pie (the Vegetables Are in It) (*see page* 119)
   Mixed Green or Combination Salad
★ Sweet Potato Pone (*see page* 183)

★ Cream of Peanut Soup (*see page* 12)
★ Florida Peanut-fed Ham Baked with Sherry
★ Corn Soufflé (*see page* 55)   (*see page* 114)
   Green Beans, Shoestring
   Brandied Peaches

★ CORNMEAL MUFFINS (*see page 25*)
RAW SHAVED CHINESE CABBAGE, FRENCH DRESSING
★ PEPPERMINT ICE CREAM (*see page 203*)

★ TURTLE SOUP (*see page 13*)
★ STEAK AND KIDNEY PIE (*see page 117*)
SCALLOPED TOMATOES
★ FRESH ORANGE SHERBET (*see page 205*)

★ BAKED SHERRIED GRAPEFRUIT (*see page 195*)
★ ROAST WILD DUCK (*see page 100*)
GIBLET GRAVY
WILD RICE
CORN MUFFINS
WILD GRAPE JELLY
★ OKRA A LA CROSS CREEK (*see page 51*)
★ BEETS IN ORANGE SAUCE (*see page 53*)
★ WHOLE WHITE ONIONS, BRAISED (*see page 54*)
★ TANGERINE SHERBET (*see page 206*)

CLEAR TOMATO SOUP
★ ALLIGATOR-TAIL STEAK (*see page 111*)
WHIPPED POTATOES
★ COW-PEAS (*see page 61*)
FRIED TOMATOES
CORNBREAD
★ AMBROSIA (*see page 195*)

CONSOMMÉ
★ VEAL CUTLET IN SHERRY (*see page 111*)

MASHED POTATOES
★ CARROT SOUFFLÉ (*see page* 54)
  BAKED TOMATOES STUFFED WITH CORN
★ HOT ROLLS (*see pages* 30, 33)
  HEAD LETTUCE, RUSSIAN DRESSING
★ GRAPE JUICE ICE CREAM (*see page* 204)

★ GREEK GULF OF MEXICO SOUP (ATHENS' KING SOUP) (*see page* 9)
★ BAKED RED SNAPPER OR SEA TROUT (*see page* 97)
★ SPANISH SAUCE (*see page* 98)
  (NO OTHER VEGETABLE NEEDED)
  AVOCADO SALAD, THE HALVES FILLED WITH GRATED CAB-
    BAGE AND ONION, FRENCH DRESSING
  CUBAN OR FRENCH BREAD, HOT
★ BAKED GUAVAS, CUSTARD SAUCE (*see page* 194)

CAMP DINNERS

  FRIED FRESH-CAUGHT ORANGE LAKE FISH
    (BREAM, PERCH OR BASS)
★ HUSH-PUPPIES (*see page* 28)
  COLE SLAW
  COFFEE
  ANY DESSERT ANY WIFE HAS THOUGHT TO BRING ALONG
    OR SEND, PREFERABLY LEMON PIE

★ ED HOPKINS' FISH CHOWDER (*see page* 96)
★ SWAMP CABBAGE (HEARTS OF PALM) RAW, WITH
    DRESSING (*see page* 64)
★ ZELMA'S ICE-BOX ROLLS (*see page* 33)

COFFEE

ANY FLORIDA FRUIT IN SEASON, WILD BLACKBERRIES, BLUE-
BERRIES, STRAWBERRIES, GRAPEFRUIT, ORANGES

★ CHICKEN, PORK, WILD DUCK, OR COOT LIVER AND GIZZARD
PILAU (*see pages* 131, 132)

★ CORN PONE (*see page* 24)

SLICED TOMATOES, CUCUMBERS AND ONIONS IN VINEGAR

COFFEE

Cross Creek Cookery

To Our Bodies' Good

I opened a letter this spring from an aviation cadet at Maxwell Field. The first sentence was startling.

"To preserve discipline in our armed forces, I demand that *Cross Creek* be banned in or near any encampment."

Of what dangerous influence was I guilty? I continued reading.

"The chapter on foods, if read by many soldiers, will wreck the morale. Our food is good, but it is not that described in 'Our Daily Bread.' My stomach is just recovering from the torture it received as a result of matter over mind."

In the next mail came a letter from a corporal. He described himself as twenty-six years old, weight two hundred and twenty-six, with a passion for food.

"Lady," he wrote, "I have never been through such agonies of frustration."

Men in the Service have written me from Hawaii, the Philip-
pines, Australia, Ireland and Egypt. Always there was a wistful
comment on my talk of foods; often a mention of a boyhood
kitchen memory. Eight out of ten letters about *Cross Creek*
ask for a recipe, or pass on a recipe, or speak of suffering over
my chat of Cross Creek dishes.

"Bless us," I thought, "the world must be hungry."

And so it is. Hungry for food and drink—not so much for
the mouth as for the mind; not for the stomach, but for the
spirit. The door of the world's house is shut and there is no
breaking of bread with the wayfarer. The frustrated corporal
wrote of his home and of his family. It was not only the
squab-sized chickens stuffed with pecans, the crab Newburg
and Dora's ice cream for which he longed, but the convivial
gathering together of folk of good will. Country foods, such as
those of Cross Creek, have in them not only Dora's cream and
butter and a dash of cooking sherry, but the peace and plenty
for which we are all homesick.

It would be inaccurate to say that I assembled this Cross
Creek Cookery "in response to wide-spread popular demand."
I needed only the slightest interest and curiosity to give me an
excuse to pass on my better dishes. Some one wrote, "Scratch a
cook and you get a recipe."

My father used to say this grace at table:

"Receive our thanks, our Heavenly Father, for these mercies.
Bless them to our bodies' good, for Thy name's sake. Amen."

Food imaginatively and lovingly prepared, and eaten in good
company, warms the being with something more than the mere
intake of calories. I cannot conceive of cooking for friends or
family, under reasonable conditions, as being a chore. Food

eaten in unpleasant circumstances is unblessed to our bodies' good—and so is a drug-store sandwich—or a raw duck. Some of my dishes, such as alligator-tail steak or Minorcan gopher stew, may horrify the delicate, who may consider them, too, unblessed. I have included nothing that is not extremely palatable, and the reader or student of culinary arts may either believe me or fall back in cowardly safety on a standard cook book.

A few recipes are not my own, or my mother's, or acquired directly at the tables of friends and relatives. These few, such as the recipe for Black Bottom pie, have proved so superlative that it would seem unkind not to share them, as they were shared with me. There are cooks who guard secret and precious recipes with their lives. This seems to me ungenerous in practitioners of an art. Occasionally a cook or housekeeper is unworthy to receive a choice recipe, and I have been known to be vague with such as these. A great many of these recipes are based on native Florida ingredients. It has been my pleasure to experiment with them, and to hang tenderly over the shoulders of Florida backwoods cooks, often sportsmen, when engaged in stirring up a dish new to me. I have served every one of the listed dishes here at Cross Creek.

In passing them on both to novitiate and to initiate, I wish that I might pass on, too, the delight of the surroundings in which they have been eaten. Whenever the Florida weather permits, which is ten or eleven months out of the year, I serve on my broad screened veranda. It faces the east, and at breakfast time the sun streams in on us, and the red birds are having breakfast too, in the feed basket in the crepe myrtle in the front yard. A dilatory feeder, more interested in his art than his maw, sings from the pecan tree that shades the veranda. At dinner-time, the sunset is rosy on the tall palm trunks in the orange grove across the yard. We have for perfume the orange blossoms in season, or the oleanders, or the tea-olive. We have for orchestra the red birds and mocking birds and doves and the susurrus of the wind in the palm trees.

In cold weather, we eat in the old-fashioned farmhouse dining room with its open fireplace. If there are only one or two guests, we are likely to have our winter breakfast on a small table in the living room by the roaring hearth fire, looking through the French windows out across the veranda to the fresh leafy world beyond.

We eat leisurely always, and sigh when we think it wise to eat no more, and know that the food will indeed be blessed to our bodies' good. Much of my "company" food is on the rich side, and I should not recommend some of the dishes for daily consumption. My friend Cecil reported to an acquaintance that after a dinner at Cross Creek, dripping with Dora's cream and butter, the guests often wandered through the old farmhouse and fell here and there on the beds to sleep. The acquaintance was horrified and avowed that such disappearances must be annoying to the hostess.

"Oh," said Cecil, "the hostess goes to sleep, too."

Where I specify Dora's cream and butter, I am indicating that so generous a quantity, of so high a quality, is meant, that one's own Jersey cow is called for. This is not always practicable or possible. In all such cases, the recipes work very nicely with ordinary materials. I mentioned to my friend Edith that I was doing a practical Cross Creek Cookery. She said, with a trace of bitterness, "You should give away a Jersey cow with every copy of the book."

Soups

I associate soup with either poverty or formal elegance. The poor make a meal of it. The elegant dabble in it, beginning a long dinner of many courses with a cup or plate of it, aggravatingly small if the soup be good, but in any case filling up a precious portion of the stomach that might better be left vacant, to my notion, for more intriguing dishes.

For a first course, if I am being rather uneasily formal and must have one, I prefer Florida grapefruit, chilled in hot weather, baked or broiled with sherry in cold, or a cup of Florida fruits in season.

Soup comes into its own, poor-man style, as a main course. One small serving of a ravishing soup is infuriating. It is like seeing the Pearly Gates swing shut in one's face after one brief glimpse of Heaven. As happy a gustatory experience as can come to mortal man, is to sit down in one of the Cuban restaurants in Tampa and eat all one can hold of Spanish bean soup, saving for another visit the Arroz con Pollo or the filet mignon Spanish style. With the soup goes the hot Cuban bread, thick and crisp of crust, delicate of interior, served hot enough to burn the fingers in six-inch portions wrapped in a paper napkin. The waiter, who looks like King Alfonso, will fill your bowl from a great silver tureen as often as it is empty; will brush off the crumbs that explode from the bread crust all over the table and bring fresh hot chunks as long as you have strength to break and butter them, and will only urge on you at the end, in your weakened condition, a trifle such as Cuban green cocoanut ice cream or guava jelly and cream cheese, with a demi-tasse of the strong Cuban coffee.

Fortunately, Cubans and Tampans are generous folk, and I have been able to bring home to the Creek backwoods the recipes for these hearty and delicious soups. Those of the mayor's wife are the best in Tampa.

There are countless pages in cook books of fine soups. I would not trespass on these, and offer here only my own favorites.

Mrs. Chancey's Spanish Bean Soup

> 1 pound Spanish beans
> ½ teaspoon soda
> 2-pound ham hock
> 4 large onions
> 4 buttons garlic
> ½ bell pepper
> 4 Spanish sausages
> 4 pig's feet (fresh)
> 4 medium-sized potatoes
> 1 small head cabbage
> ½ teaspoon saffron (or about 10¢ worth)
> Salt to taste
> Black pepper to taste
> 2 bay leaves

Add soda to water and soak beans overnight. Wash beans well the next morning.

Cover ham hock well with cold water, add beans and start cooking slowly. Cut up onions, garlic, bell pepper, and in about twenty minutes add to soup together with bay leaves and saffron. Cut sausages in pieces of four each and add to soup. Cut pig's feet in half, lengthwise, and cook separately until tender; then add to soup and cook slowly. Cut up potatoes and add to soup, and when beans are about done, cut up cabbage as for slaw and add to soup. Season to taste with salt and black pepper.

Be sure to cook slowly always. More water may be needed at end, but soup is supposed to be very thick. Imported sausage cannot be bought now but domestic will do. Serves eight to ten.

Mrs. Chancey's Black Bean Soup

1 pound black beans
½ teaspoon soda
1 cup olive oil
3 onions
3 buttons garlic
½ bell pepper
4 strips breakfast bacon
2 bay leaves
1 tablespoon vinegar
Salt to taste
Pepper to taste

Add soda to water and soak beans overnight. Wash beans well the next morning.

Put beans in two quarts of cold water and boil slowly. Cut up onions, garlic, bell pepper, bacon and bay leaves and put into frying pan with olive oil and fry until light brown. Add this mixture, together with vinegar, to the beans and cook slowly until done. Season to taste. Serves eight.

Beans should set about an hour or two before eating. Re-heat. Serve with side dishes of rice and chopped onions, to be added to the soup to individual taste.

Not far from Tampa is Tarpon Springs, that unique colony of Greek sponge divers that has set up a corner of the Old World in the New. To the Creek were brought me by Chuck Rawlings, who lived and sailed with the Greek spongers, two superb Greek recipes for soup for which my own section also provides the ingredients.

Greek Gulf of Mexico Soup
(Athens' King Soup)

2 medium-sized onions
2 green peppers
1 heart of celery
2 ripe tomatoes
½ cup olive oil
Seasoning of Greek origanon (thyme), salt, pepper
4 to 6 cups hot water, according to amount of fish
Large, firm, meaty fish, preferably red snapper
1¼ cups spaghetti points or vermacelli
2 eggs well beaten
Juice of 2 lemons

Cook vegetables in olive oil slowly, until soft. Add seasonings and hot water. Simmer until vegetables are thoroughly tender. Add fish cut in large pieces, including the head. Simmer about ten minutes, or until just tender—not too long. Remove the fish (the meat may be served separately with lemon butter or Béchamel, Anchovy, Béarnaise or Tyrolienne sauce). Add spaghetti points or vermicelli to soup and simmer fifteen minutes. Add slowly to eggs well beaten with lemon juice. Serves six to eight.

Greek Lemon Soup

3 cups beef stock
1 small onion
or
1 clove garlic
Salt and pepper to taste
2 eggs, well beaten
Juice of 1 lemon
½ cup cooked rice

Slice onion very thin, or mince the garlic, and simmer until tender in the strained beef stock. Canned beef bouillon may be used, but home-made stock is better. Onion or garlic may be strained out if preferred. Stir in cooked rice and let stock come to a boil. Pour boiling stock over well beaten eggs and lemon juice. Float a wafer-thin slice of lemon sprinkled with minced parsley on top of each serving. Serves four to six.

Chef Huston's
Cream of Cucumber Soup (Potage Cumberlan

1 large or 2 medium cucumbers
4 tablespoons butter
2 tablespoons flour
1 quart whole milk, hot
Salt

Wash and grate, without peeling, cucumbers on coarse side of grater. Sauté in butter until golden brown, add flour, salt to taste, and whole hot milk, blending until smooth. Strain if pre-ferred. One-half tablespoon grated onion may be sautéed with the cucumber, but this interferes with the subtle flavor. Top with one teaspoon whipped cream to each serving. Serves six to eight.

Ruth Becker's Creole Oyster Soup

1 quart oysters
3 pints water
3 to 5 cloves garlic
4 or 5 onions
¼ lb. butter
3 tablespoons flour
Salt
Pepper
Tabasco
Coarse thyme
2 bay leaves
1 pint thin cream

Place oysters and cold water in a kettle. Cut up garlic and onions very fine. Brown lightly in butter, and stir in the flour. Add to oysters and water. Simmer, tightly covered, for three hours. Add seasonings to taste, but never omit the bay leaves. Add thin cream. Serve at once. This is a superb recipe. Serves six generously.

Chef Huston's Cream of Peanut Soup (Potage Dixie)

2 tablespoons flour
1 tablespoon butter
1 quart whole milk, hot
1 cup peanut butter
Salt to taste
1 jigger dry sherry

Make a roux of butter and flour. Stir in slowly the hot milk, and blend until smooth. Stir in peanut butter, blending. When ready to serve, add the sherry. Top each serving with a teaspoon of whipped cream. This is unbelievably delicate. Serves eight.

Onion Soup Au Gratin

2 cups sliced onions
½ tablespoon Karo syrup
3 tablespoons Wesson oil
5 cups brown soup stock (any kind)
1 tablespoon cornstarch
6 large squares toasted bread
¾ cup grated cheese

Cook onions in Karo syrup and Wesson oil until soft and tender. Add cornstarch, stirring well, stock, salt and pepper. Bring to a boil, place square of toast in each individual soup dish, ladle out the boiling soup and sprinkle thickly with the grated cheese. Serves six to eight.

Florida Soft-Shell Turtle Soup
(Cooter)

The soft-shell cooter is a brown, flat, pancake-like turtle found in Florida fresh water. The meat has a fine flavor, much like a diamond-back terrapin or a deep-sea turtle. This soup is as good as any expensive green turtle soup.

> 1 cooter (there should be about 3 lbs. of meat)
> 3 quarts water
> 12 whole cloves
> 12 whole allspice
> Salt and pepper
> Browned flour, about 4 tablespoons
> ½ cup sherry
> Nutmeg, grated
> Lemon slices
> Hard-boiled eggs or turtle eggs

Cut away the shell of the cooter. Cut out the meat, saving the eggs separately, if any. Scald the feet and rub off skin. Scald and skin soft, gelatinous outer edge of shell. Cut in pieces. Cover the meat and feet with water, adding cloves, allspice, salt and pepper. Simmer for three or four hours. Some Southern cooks serve the meat and spices in the soup but I prefer to remove them. (The meat may be dipped in egg batter and deep fried.) I cut one cup of the soft shell in one-half-inch cubes and return to the soup. Thicken with browned flour. Soup should be on the thin side. If there were eggs in the turtle, and if the assembled guests are known to like them, break the eggs and drop into the soup and simmer fifteen minutes. Otherwise place two or three thin slices of hard-boiled egg in each soup plate. Just before serving, add the sherry. On each serving float a slice of lemon and dust lightly with grated nutmeg. Serves eight.

Cream of Fordhook Soup

2 cups white stock, or
2 small cans chicken consommé
2 cups shelled fresh Fordhooks (lima beans)
1 cup scalded rich milk
2 tablespoons flour
2 tablespoons butter
Salt and pepper
1 tablespoon fresh onion juice

Cook beans in boiling salted water to cover until tender, allowing water to cook away. Put through sieve. Melt butter, stir in flour, add scalded milk, then white stock, blending until smooth. Add salt and pepper to taste. Stir in sieved beans, adding onion juice. Place a dot of butter on each serving and sprinkle lightly with paprika. Serves four to six.

Crab Soup

This is powerful good, but to my notion, a waste of fresh crab-meat unless one happens to have an abundance, or has a passion for soups.

8 crabs
2 cups milk
1 cup cream
2 tablespoons butter
1 tablespoon flour
Salt, black pepper, cayenne
1 very small onion, minced
2 sprigs parsley finely chopped
2 tablespoons sherry

Plunge crabs into boiling, salted water and cook rapidly for twenty minutes. Cool. Pick out the crab meat and separate into flakes. Place butter, crab meat and minced onion together in the top of a double boiler. Sauté over very low flame for five minutes. Add one and three-quarters cups of the milk, heated, to the mixture, salt, black pepper and cayenne to taste. Mix flour in remaining one-quarter cup of cold milk, and stir into mixture. Simmer over very low flame for five minutes, being careful to avoid scorching, then place over bottom part of double boiler with boiling water and cook, covered, thirty minutes more. Stir in cream slowly, and parsley. When piping hot, add the sherry, and serve. Serve with hot Cuban bread or pulled bread. At the season when female crabs are available, the eggs should be removed before cooking the crabs, and added to the soup at the time the milk is added. Canned crab-meat may be used. Serves six.

Chicken Soup with Baby Dumplings

Boil one fowl, whole, in water to cover. Add two stalks celery, including leaves, one teaspoon salt and one tablespoon cider vinegar. Boil rapidly for twenty minutes, then reduce heat to simmering. Cook for four and one-half hours or until meat falls from bones. Remove fowl and celery stalks. There should be eight cups of broth. Skim off excess fat. Add more salt to taste. Make dumplings of one and one-half cups flour sifted with two teaspoons baking powder, one-half teaspoon salt. Combine one beaten egg and one-half cup milk and stir into dry ingredients. Drop into boiling soup by half-teaspoons, cover tightly, reduce heat to a slow boil, and steam for ten minutes. The meat of the fowl may be utilized for chicken croquettes. Serves eight to ten.

Donax Broth

Midway between high and low tide along the Florida coasts— and perhaps along other coasts, too—there bubble up from the sand the diminutive clam-like molluscs called Donax. We also call them periwinkles, inaccurately, of course, and the multi-colored pastel shells are the substance of our coquina rock, used by the Spaniards in much of the old St. Augustine construction. Gathering the Donax is a race against time and tide, for they appear only briefly. We scoop them into sieves or colanders, washing out the sand in the surf as we go. It takes about six quarts of Donax to make a quart of broth. After washing well, do not quite cover with cold water. Cover the kettle and bring slowly to a simmer, stirring every now and then. The tiny molluscs pop open and the sweet clam-like juice adds itself to the water to make a delicate and delicious broth. When the kettle reaches the boiling point, let simmer several minutes, stirring twice. Drain immediately. The broth needs no salt. It may be chilled in the ice-box and served clear as a cold and re-freshing consommé. I like it best with two tablespoons thin cream and a small lump of butter added to each serving, and served piping hot.

With all these soups, I prefer Cuban bread or pulled toasted bread, with plenty of Dora's butter, to the crackers of commerce and convention. A light salad may follow, if the soup alone seems meagre. The lightest of

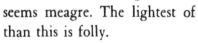

than this is folly.

Hot Breads

A stranger who meant to be kind wrote me a "fan letter" about one of my books. We had a mutual acquaintance, it seemed, and of this acquaintance my correspondent had inquired as to my appearance. The answer was, "She looks like a woman who is a good cook and enjoys her own cooking." A. J. Cronin, that presumably saintly author of *The Keys of the Kingdom,* questioned my ability to go off into the backwoods with a Dutch oven and emerge with "an Emily Post dinner for twelve." He called me "a plump impostor." If these brutal descriptions be true, the cause is undoubtedly Southern hot breads.

It is better to be plump than to live on baker's bread. We call it "light bread" at the Creek, and a friend from the Big Scrub goes an intelligent step farther and calls it "wasp-nest bread." It is an old tale that the South is known as the land of the hot biscuit and the cold check. Yet a part of the placidity of the South comes from the sense of well-being that follows the heart-and-body-warming consumption of breads fresh from the oven. We serve cold baker's bread only to our enemies, trusting that they will never impose on our hospitality again. A female Northern friend of mine married a male Kentucky friend of mine. She refused at first to be bothered with the hours-long trouble of making Kentucky beaten biscuits. Just as the marriage was about to go on the rocks, and rightly, she saw the light. Beaten biscuits now hold the happy household together. I offer no recipe for them, as they are not a part of Creek life. I refer the wise curious to the Duchess of Windsor's fine book, *My Favorite Southern Recipes*. She calls them Maryland Beaten Biscuit, but it is all the same.

There are two varieties of Florida hot biscuits. The backwoods variety is thick, substantial, and very good for the extremely hungry. It is not my choice, except when I join a rural family after a hunt, or on a camping trip, but I offer it for its filling value.

Florida Backwoods Biscuits

Almost every Florida country kitchen has an old-fashioned kitchen safe. On top of this usually sits a small dishpan or large, old-fashioned milk pan, partly filled with self-rising flour. Once or twice a day the pan is taken down and placed on the kitchen table, a little hollow scooped in the center, and home-made lard and water, or milk and water, mixed in, flour being gathered from the sides of the pan as the cook works. This is apparently a hit-or-miss process, but of course the experienced cook subconsciously measures with hand and eye. The biscuits are shaped by hand from the mixed dough in the center of the pan.

Idella and I think that we improve on most backwoods biscuits. We use regular flour instead of self-rising, use probably more shortening, and mix in ordinary fashion in a bowl, measuring as we go.

> 1½ cups flour sifted with
> 2 teaspoons baking powder
> ½ teaspoon salt
> Mix in with fingers
> 2 tablespoons Crisco
> Cut in with knife or fork
> ⅓ cup milk

Roll out on floured board, fold over twice, rolling, and have dough one-half inch in thickness. Cut large rounds with a water tumbler or doughnut cutter. Bake fifteen to twenty minutes in a hot oven—four hundred and fifty degrees. Serves three to four.

I am torn between the type of biscuits made by my mother and my grandmother and by me, before I became a Floridian, and the biscuits made by the best of Negro cooks. My family sort is fluffy, tender, falling apart in layers.

Mother's Biscuits

2 cups flour
5 teaspoons baking powder
2 tablespoons butter
1 cup milk (scant)
½ teaspoon salt

Mix dry ingredients and sift twice. Work in butter with tips of fingers. Add milk gradually, cutting in with knife to make a soft dough. Amount of milk needed will vary according to flour. Only enough should be used to hold the dough together. It is supposed to be heresy to handle biscuit dough needlessly, but to make flaky, layered biscuits, roll out the dough, then fold it over on itself in four layers, as though making pie crust. Roll out to a thickness of one-half inch and cut wih a biscuit cutter. Bake about twelve minutes in a hot oven—four hundred and fifty degrees.

This is a good basic recipe for making quick cinnamon buns. Sprinkle the dough with brown sugar, cinnamon, dots of butter, raisins and or nuts if desired. Roll up like a jelly roll. Cut off three-quarter-inch slices, place in buttered tins and bake fifteen minutes in a hot oven. Serves four.

The sort made by all the colored cooks I have had is as crisp as Scotch short-bread, well-browned and small, and melting on the tongue. It is the perfect biscuit for serving with any heavy meal.

Idella's Crisp Biscuits

2 cups flour
4 teaspoons baking powder
¾ teaspoon salt
6 tablespoons Crisco or butter
¾ cup milk
Serves 4

Mix as usual, using a fork throughout. Roll out once, to a thickness of one-quarter inch. Cut in very small rounds, one inch in diameter. Bake twelve or fifteen minutes in a very hot oven. These are so crisp and thin that they are usually eaten by placing a dab of butter on top without attempting to split the biscuit, and making one or two bites of it. Men love them, but are likely to be embarrassed by them, as they are ashamed to keep asking for them. I always say, "Oh, take several," and keep a plate on the table.

I told a tale in *Cross Creek* that sounds like one of Irvin Cobb's yarns, of a Northerner who visited the South and never got to taste a hot Southern biscuit. He was a great talker, and as the maid passed the biscuits he would take one, butter it, put it down, and launch into conversation. Reaching for his biscuit, his hostess would say, "Oh, no! You must have a hot one." She would ring for the maid and the biscuits, the guest would take one, butter it, put it down, give forth, only to have his biscuit snatched from him as he was ready for it. As the tale goes, he left the South without experiencing one of its greatest delights.

"Bread" to the Floridian is cornbread. This is as it should be, for corn is plentiful, it may be bought cheaply when not raised on the place, and may be bought "water-ground" or taken to some local mill for grinding. Until recently, no Florida farm or clearing was complete without its own stone for corn grinding, and on the clearing in the Florida Scrub that I used in my mind as the site of Baxter's Island in *The Yearling,* there still stand the upper and nether millstone turned by a hand crank for making the sweet, fresh cornmeal that makes of cornbread a delectable staple.

There are infinite gradations of cornbread, from the hoe-cake of slavery and Civil War times, when the Negroes baked it on hoes before an open flame and the soldiers baked it on their bayonets before the bivouac fires, up to the melting softness of spoonbread. Here are the gradations, from low to high, all good according to the moment's need.

I do not know whether other Southern cooks would agree with me, but I draw a line between hoe cake and corn pone.

Hoe Cake

1 cup white cornmeal,
    preferably water-ground
½ teaspoon salt
Boiling water
Serves 3 to 4

Mix salt and cornmeal. Pour into it, stirring constantly, enough boiling water to make a batter that just holds together, without spreading when placed on the griddle. Have iron griddle or skillet hot but not smoking, grease with bacon rind or bacon fat. Spread batter in one large cake or in smaller cakes three to four inches in diameter, to a thickness of one-half inch. Cook very slowly, turning when well-browned and brown on the other side. This is very much a primitive and fundamental "bread," but the flavor is sweet and nutty, the texture rather ingratiating. The batter may be made thinner, spread on the griddle to a thickness of only one-quarter inch, and in very small cakes, two inches in diameter. These make a good crisp bread for a country or a camp breakfast, served with sausage, ham or bacon. It is good served with butter and Southern cane syrup, for those with a sweet tooth.

Corn Pone

Corn pone is hoe cake dressed up a little. One-half cup of flour is used for every cup of cornmeal, a little more salt, milk, or part milk and water used instead of water, two teaspoons of baking powder added for every one and one-half cups of the dry mixture, if sweet milk is used, or one-half teaspoon soda if sour milk or buttermilk. The milk or milk and water is not heated for corn pone. Two tablespoons of melted shortening are added after mixing the other ingredients. Country folk use the fat from white bacon (salt pork), but I prefer a vegetable shortening such as Crisco. The pone is cooked in a deep iron skillet over a slow flame, the batter, just thick enough to hold together, is spread to a depth of one to one and one-half inches, the pone flipped over when well browned on one side, and browned very slowly on the other. It is cut in triangular pieces like pie.

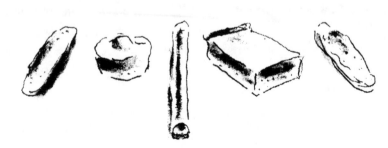

Oven Cornbread

1 cup flour
1 cup cornmeal
½ teaspoon salt
4 teaspoons baking powder
¾ cup milk
1 egg
¼ cup melted butter or Crisco

Sift together flour, cornmeal, salt and baking powder. Stir in milk (quantity needed will vary a little—the batter should be on the thin side), then the egg, well beaten, beat briskly a couple of minutes, stir in melted shortening and bake in a moderate to hot oven about thirty minutes. Sour milk or buttermilk may be used instead of sweet milk, in which case use a fraction over one-half teaspoon of soda instead of baking powder, and bake slowly. Serves four.

Cornmeal Muffins

1¼ cups flour
¾ cup cornmeal
½ teaspoon salt
4 teaspoons baking powder
2 tablespoons sugar
¾ cup milk
2 eggs
¼ cup melted butter

Mix as for cornbread. Bake in well greased muffin pans in a hot oven about twenty-five minutes. Serves four.

Aunt Effie's Custard Johnny Cake

1 cup buttermilk
1 cup sweet milk
2 eggs
2 tablespoons sugar
1 teaspoon soda
1 teaspoon salt
1 cup cornmeal
½ cup flour

Mix and sift together the cornmeal, flour, soda, salt and sugar. Beat in the buttermilk, then stir in the well-beaten eggs. Add the sweet milk last, blending quickly. Pour into a greased rectangular pan and bake in a hot oven about thirty-five minutes. Serve immediately, cutting in squares at the table. The custard will rise to the top in baking. Serves four to six.

Spoonbread

I think I never ate a poor spoonbread. Most of the good recipes are similar, the variance being largely in the number of eggs.

1 cup cornmeal
1 cup boiling water
2 cups rich milk
1 teaspoon salt
1 tablespoon melted butter
2 or 3 eggs
1½ teaspoons baking powder
Serves 4

Scald cornmeal with boiling water. Let cool, stirring to prevent lumping. Add milk slowly, mixed with salt and baking powder, well-beaten eggs, and last, melted butter. Pour into well-buttered baking pan and bake about forty minutes in a moderate oven three hundred and seventy-five degrees. Spoonbreads and custard cornbreads should be served in the pan in which they are baked. A napkin may be folded around the pan if it is not suitable for a public appearance.

Crackling Bread

"Crackling bread" does not refer to the "shortenin' bread" against which our stomachs have been turned by parlor-loads of amateur baritones, bellowing "Mama's little baby—," usually without benefit even of piano. It is tied up definitely, however, with the hog-killing season, for cracklings are the crisp, nutty residue left from making home-made lard. The fat is cut into small squares for trying out, and each square is apotheosized into a brown crinkled kernel that turns po' folks' cornbread in the autumn into a delicacy unobtainable in high places.

> 2 cups water-ground cornmeal
> 1 teaspoon salt
> 3 teaspoons baking powder
> ½ cup skimmed milk
> ½ cup water
> 1 egg
> ½ cup cracklings
> Serves 4

Mix and sift dry ingredients. Stir in milk and water and beat until smooth. Drop in egg and beat again. Stir in cracklings and bake in a lightly greased iron skillet about thirty minutes in a hot oven, about four hundred degrees. If the cracklings are no larger than a pea, I stir them in whole. Otherwise, I break up the larger pieces. Some cooks crush the cracklings with a rolling pin, but this makes them too fine for my taste. There is no point in having cracklings, and then disguising them.

Hush-puppies are in a class by themselves. They are a concomitant of the hunt, above all of the fishing trip. Fresh-caught fried fish without hush puppies are as man without woman, a beautiful woman without kindness, law without policemen. The story goes that they derived their name from old fishing and hunting expeditions, when the white folks ate to repletion, the Negro help ate beyond repletion, and the hunting dogs, already fed, smelled the delectable odors of human rations and howled for the things they scented. Negro cook or white sportsman tossed the remaining cornmeal patties to the dogs, calling, "Hush, puppies!"—and the dogs, devouring them, could ask no more of life, and hushed.

Hush-Puppies

> 1 cup cornmeal
> 2 teaspoons baking powder
> ½ teaspoon salt
> 1 small to medium onion, minced
> 1 egg
> ¼ cup milk or water
> Serves 3 to 4

Mix together the dry ingredients and the finely cut onion. Break in the egg and beat vigorously. Add the liquid. Form into small patties, round or finger-shaped. Drop in the deep smoking fat in which the fish has been fried, until they are a deep brown. Serve hot and at once.

I have a strange recipe from St. Simon's Island, off the coast of Georgia, that adds a little sugar and a small can of corn to hush-puppies. Sugar is anathema in any cornbread except the most delicate cornmeal muffins. It is more than inappropriate to the hearty honesty of hush-puppies. As to the canned corn, this is a free country and the experimenter may legally add it if he so wishes. He may not legally, however, then call the results hush-puppies.

From a rural correspondent I had passed on one of those flashes of genius that touch cooking at fortunate moments. His mother, he wrote, made hush-puppies in small round cakes about two inches in diameter, then with her finger poked a hole in the center, as for a doughnut. This gives twice the amount of crisp, crunchy crust, the very best part of the hush-puppy, and does away with any tendency to a heavy center. I recommend it earnestly.

I do not recommend a practice of some sportsmen, of using beer for the mixing fluid. By it, the sweet nutty flavor of the hush-puppy is a little soured, even when baking soda is used instead of baking powder. Devotees of this custom are likely to be those so unbalanced by large quantities of the mixing fluid that they are in no condition to treat hush-puppies with the respect due them.

Two recipes for rolls have played a part in my life. The first is almost certainly responsible for my later years as a cook, for it was in learning to make superb Parker House rolls when in cooking school at the age of twelve, that I first knew the delights of culinary acclaim. I still have, somewhat damaged by Florida cockroaches, my class cook-book of that early era. The handwriting is round and childish and the teacher's penciled marks were always "Very Good" or "Excellent." The making of the Parker House rolls at home was an appallingly messy procedure, for I kept the kitchen littered for the day and a half necessary to complete them. My mother, a magnificent cook, like her mother before her, discouraged my ventures into the domestic arts through a mistaken idea that they were ignoble. She permitted the Parker House rolls only, I think, because it seemed an amusing accomplishment for a child. It is still a good recipe.

Parker House Rolls

1 pint milk
2 teaspoons salt
4 tablespoons butter
4 tablespoons sugar
½ yeast cake dissolved in
½ cup lukewarm water
1 egg
Flour to make a soft dough (about 6 cups)

To the scalded milk add the salt, sugar and butter. Stir until the butter is melted. Let cool until lukewarm. Add the dissolved yeast. Add one-half the flour, about three cups, sifted, or enough to make a drop batter. (Only experience teaches a cook certain simple things. A drop batter is one that will drop off from the spoon without running. A batter with too much flour in it will also drop off in a lump. It becomes drop batter when just enough flour has been added to make it drop, for the first time.) Let this stand in the covered mixing bowl from one to two hours. Add the egg, well beaten, and enough flour to make a soft dough. One secret of these rolls is in using no more flour than is necessary for handling. Turn out on a well-floured board and knead until smooth and elastic. Place in a greased mixing bowl, grease the surface, cover well, and let stand in a warm place until it has doubled in bulk.

Cut off one section of dough at a time and work up into rolls. Knead each section again on a floured board and roll out to a thickness of one-half inch. Cut rounds with a doughnut cutter or water tumbler. With the dull edge of a table knife, crease each round across the center. Butter one half-moon side with soft but not melted butter. Fold over and pinch the open edges tightly together. Place one inch apart, if plenty of crust is preferred, in buttered pans. Brush melted butter lightly over the tops. Place uncovered in a warm place, without draughts, until doubled in bulk and light and puffy. Bake twenty to twenty-five minutes in a hot oven.

I make delicious cinnamon buns from this mixture by rolling out a section of the dough to one-quarter or three-eighths inch thickness, spreading with soft butter, brown sugar, powdered cinnamon, raisins, and nuts if desired. Roll up like a jelly roll and cut off slices one inch thick. Place with the cut side up in a buttered pan, let raise until puffy, and bake in a slightly slower oven, about three hundred and seventy-five degrees. Serve or turn out immediately, or they will stick to the pan.

This is a recipe for a sizeable family, but the rolls warm up nicely, and the cinnamon buns keep well.

The other recipe for rolls comes from my friend Zelma, the local census-taker. It came into my life along with my friendship with her and with Ed Hopkins of the Dutch oven, the fish chowder and the turtle dishes, at a time when the delights of Florida woods and streams were fresh and new. It is as simple a recipe as I know for raised rolls, as delicious, as convenient. The mixture may be kept in the ice-box as long as ten days, ready at hand for serving hot rolls on an hour's notice. It reaches its perfection when baked out of doors in a Dutch oven. Cast iron has never been improved on for cooking. Let no modern cook feel pity for our fore-mothers who baked their breads and their meats in a Dutch oven on an open hearth. The Dutch oven is of varying sizes, made with three legs for sitting evenly over hot coals, a long handle for lifting, and a tight lid indented to a depth of about an inch and a half. On this lid are scattered hot hardwood coals. Only practice can determine the amount of coals and the degree of heat necessary under and on the oven. The inexpert might safely bake cornbread in a Dutch oven. Only the expert dare attempt the baking of Zelma's rolls. They must bake neither too fast nor too slow. They must emerge oak-brown of crust on all sides, meltingly light and fluffy and thoroughly done within. An ordinary oven will serve if necessary. The heat in this case should be three hundred and seventy-five degrees for thirty minutes, increasing the last ten if needed for good browning.

Zelma's Ice Box Rolls

1 cup hot mashed potatoes
Stir in 1 cup sugar until smooth
Add 1 cup of the hot potato water, and
1 cup cold water
Cool until lukewarm
Add 1 yeast cake dissolved in
½ cup lukewarm water

Let mixture stand five hours, covered. Then place in the ice box, and rolls may be made from it on short notice. The basic mixture keeps well about a week.

To make the rolls, enough for about four people, beat one egg in a measuring cup. Fill the cup with the basic mixture. Turn into a mixing bowl and add one teaspoon salt, one-third cup melted shortening, then two cups flour, sifted. The rolls may be shaped by hand directly from the bowl, without kneading. Or the dough may be rolled out on a floured board and made into Parker House rolls. More flour will be necessary in handling.

Man cannot live by cornbread and raised rolls alone. I list other hot breads that disappear so rapidly from off my table at the Creek that I feel certain they must have merit.

Breakfast Muffins

¼ cup butter (or Crisco)
¼ cup sugar
½ teaspoon salt
1 egg
1 cup milk
2 cups flour
5 teaspoons baking powder

Cream butter and sugar together until light. Add egg well beaten. Sift together flour, baking powder and salt, and add to the first mixture alternately with the milk. Bake twenty-five minutes in buttered muffin pans in a hot oven. Makes twelve large muffins.

Idella's Luncheon Muffins

⅓ cup butter or Crisco
⅓ cup sugar
1 egg
½ cup milk (scant)
1½ cups flour
3 teaspoons baking powder
¼ teaspoon salt

Mix like breakfast muffins, but bake in tiny muffin pans. Makes about eighteen small muffins.

These are much richer and sweeter than mine, delicious for a party luncheon, but do not warm up well for the next morning's breakfast, due to their shortness.

Sour Cream Muffins

(courtesy of Dora)

2 cups flour
1 tablespoon sugar
3 teaspoons baking powder
1 teaspoon salt (scant)
1 teaspoon soda
1 egg
1½ cups Dora's sour cream

Sift together the flour, baking powder, salt and sugar. Add half of the cream, stirring lightly. Stir in the soda dissolved in two tablespoons of the cream, then the beaten egg. Add the remainder of the cream and beat well. Bake twenty minutes in a hot oven, four hundred and fifty degrees. This makes one dozen utterly delicious large muffins, or two dozen small ones.

Sour Cream Pancakes

1¾ cups flour
¾ teaspoon salt
1 teaspoon soda
1½ cups Dora's sour cream
1 egg
1 tablespoon sugar

Mix and sift dry ingredients. Add sour cream, then egg well beaten. Bake on a greased hot griddle. Serves three to four.

Thin Cornmeal Pancakes

½ cup cornmeal
½ teaspoon salt
1 tablespoon sugar
½ cup boiling water
Mix slowly, beating well
Add in order
½ cup flour
3 teaspoons baking powder
¼ cup milk
¼ cup melted shortening
1 well beaten egg
Serves 3

Bake more slowly than for flour pancakes, as they have a tendency to brown before being done.

Waffles

2 cups flour
1 teaspoon salt
5 teaspoons baking powder
2 tablespoons sugar
1 cup milk
2 eggs
⅔ cup melted shortening (melted Crisco
　　or Wesson oil)
Serves 4 generously

Mix and sift dry ingredients. Stir in milk slowly, beating well. Amount of milk needed will vary. The batter should be thinner than for pancakes. Add eggs well beaten, then melted shortening. Shortening should be cooled a little before adding to the batter. Pour from a pitcher into smoking hot waffle irons. Waffles are best when made at the table and eaten at once. When a cook in the kitchen attempts to bake enough at one time for a family, and is obliged to cover them to keep them hot, they become soft and tough, instead of crisp and tender.

The fault in most poor, heavy waffles, is lack of enough shortening. Note the large amount in this recipe, which makes crisp, light waffles, good either as a breakfast dish or served with creamed chicken for luncheon or supper.

Thin Bread Pancakes

1 cup stale bread crumbs
1 cup milk
1 egg
¼ cup flour
½ teaspoon salt
3 teaspoons baking powder
2 tablespoons melted butter
Serves 3

Soak bread crumbs—I like them rather coarse—in milk overnight in ice box if possible, or for an hour or so. Add egg well beaten, flour sifted with salt and baking powder, then melted butter. Bake on a well-greased smoking hot griddle in very small griddle cakes, as they are difficult to turn when large.

Luncheon Dishes
or,
The Embroidery Club

Several of my finest recipes are for luncheon dishes. These came from the Embroidery Club, and I never prepare a company luncheon without wondering whether the members of that organization, many of them dead and gone, would have Oh-ed and Ah-ed discreetly, attempting to disguise their Victorian greediness.

Mother was some time in being invited to join the Embroidery Club, and I think that Aunt Jenny, a charter member, dangled it before her nose so that she should be properly grateful when the great moment came. After having been several times a guest, Mother's appreciation of good food, her embroidery and her general acceptability were finally approved, and the day came when it was her week to entertain. The ladies used "Embroidery" as an excuse for their weekly meetings, but although a certain amount of cut-work doilies was eventually completed, a certain amount of hand-embroidered pillow-slips, tea-aprons and utterly useless and indefinable knick-knacks meant for Christmas presents, the real purpose of the Embroidery Club was to eat. This they did with a twittering and a gusto that would have left the plates and platters clean if the mode had not been to provide more than could possibly be eaten. Our own suppers or dinners on Mother's day were a continuation of the noon's luncheon, and I looked forward to these with unholy zeal. Mother herself was usually unable farther to partake, ill in bed with a sick headache, brought on by the nervous tension caused by trying to outdo the previous eleven Embroidery Club luncheons.

Let not the suspicious dismiss Mother's egg croquettes and jellied chicken without trying them, in the belief that they are so simple that they cannot be exceptional. Some of the most delicate dishes in the world are of pristine simplicity, but with a subtle flavor past the most elaborate French concoctions. I am here offering her egg croquettes for the first time, having withheld them for fear they should fall into the hands of the unworthy.

I did give the recipe to my husband's chef for his Castle Warden Hotel, and was secretly delighted when the croquettes were not as good as mine. He made them too small and dipped them twice in egg and crumbs, which made too thick a crust.

I did have it slipped from under my nose by my dearest friend, whom I had evaded on the subject for the reason that she herself would not go near the kitchen, but left all to any passing cook. It seemed to me that the dish should be made with loving hands or not at all. My friend was caught in the great Kentucky flood and I invited her and her children to stay with me at the Creek until she could return to her home. She brought, on vacation, her cook of the moment, who slyly watched me prepare the croquettes. It seemed that the Louisville Country Club also serves a delicious egg croquette, whose ingredients it guards with its life. My friend expected to return to Louisville and flaunt the dish. I was again delighted when she later reported the theft of my recipe, and that the results were not quite right.

Mother's Egg Croquettes

7 hard-boiled eggs
3 tablespoons butter
4 tablespoons flour
½ or ¾ teaspoon salt, to taste
1 cup milk
1 very small onion
4 sprigs parsley
Serves 4 to 5

Peel the hard-boiled eggs and put them through the meat grinder, along with the onion and parsley. Make a very thick cream sauce of the butter, flour, salt and milk. Sauce this thick is hard to handle, and must be beaten until smooth. Add the ground eggs and onion and parsley to the hot cream sauce. Let cool, then place the skillet in the ice box to chill the mixture thoroughly. I usually make the mixture several hours before using it. Mould the mixture into croquettes. This quantity makes ten. Return croquettes, placed on wax paper, to the ice box to chill again. When ready to fry, dip quickly in slightly beaten whole egg, then roll in fine bread crumbs. The croquettes are soft and hard to handle, but there will be no damage done in handling quickly. Fry in a basket in deep smoking hot fat until a rich brown. Do not crowd croquettes in basket, as contact makes them burst open. Serve at once.

Mother's Jellied Chicken

Boil a whole, dressed chicken, about three and one-half pounds, in enough water to cover, until very tender. Remove the chicken and boil the liquor down to one quart. Cut the meat in small pieces, cutting across the grain to give square or rectangular pieces rather than shredded fragments. Discard any portions of skin that may be too coarse. Season the meat lightly with salt and pepper. To the quart of hot stock, add two tablespoons gelatine soaked in two tablespoons of cold water, one tablespoon Worcestershire sauce, and more salt to taste. Strain the stock over the chicken, mix lightly but thoroughly, and put into a fancy mould or into a long deep rectangular loaf tin. Cool, and chill in ice box until set. Serve on lettuce with mayonnaise on the side. Serves eight generously.

The secret of the goodness of this jellied chicken is its very simplicity. I have had jellied chicken fixed up with an assortment of celery, cucumber, carrots, hard-boiled eggs and green peppers and pimentos and what-not. All these alien and dressy ingredients destroy the melting flavor.

Mother's Embroidery Club luncheon dishes are likely to appear at the Creek as supper dishes. I seldom have guests for luncheon, for two reasons; my habits of work are known to considerate friends, and they prefer to come out from town in the cool of the evening, knowing that work is over and the hospitable mood upon me. A car driving up to the gate in the middle of the day produces muffled curses. The same car arriving as the sun is dropping over Orange Lake is welcomed with unqualified joy. I rush with my dog in greeting to the gate, scurry to the ice box to prepare drinks, and take a quick look within to decide of what the evening meal shall consist. Since there is no telephone, praise be to God, at the Creek, I try always to be prepared for unexpected supper guests.

The egg croquettes, of course, can only be served on advance notice or invitation. The jellied chicken is perfect for an on-hand delicacy. I make a good individual creamed chicken salad and a jellied tongue that are ideal for my purposes. Salmon loaf may be made on short notice. I keep good medium strong cheese always on hand, and Idella's cheese soufflé, with hot muffins and a salad, makes as pleasant a supper as one can ask. There are always plenty of eggs in the ice box, canned fruits in the pantry, citrus on the trees, and rum in the liquor cupboard, and a rum omelet sending up blue flames to match the flicker of fireflies in the orange grove is a delight to eye and palate. And I always have pecans for pecan patties.

Jellied Tongue

1 small or medium-sized fresh beef tongue
1 stalk celery
1 slice of onion
2 bay leaves
6 whole cloves
6 whole allspice
2 tablespoons vinegar
1 teaspoon salt
1 cup to 1 can beef consommé
1 tablespoon gelatine
3 to 5 hard-boiled eggs
1 tablespoon Worcestershire sauce
Serves 6 generously

Boil tongue slowly in cold water to cover well, adding all the seasonings except Worcestershire. When tender, in two to two and one-half hours, turn out fire and let tongue cool in the broth. Peel tongue and cut out any small bones or coarse particles at the thick end. Cut in slices lengthwise and put through the meat grinder. Put the hard-boiled eggs through the meat grinder. Mix with the ground tongue. The number of eggs and the amount of consommé depend on the size of the tongue. Soak gelatine in two tablespoons of the cold consommé. Heat the rest of the consommé to boiling and pour over the gelatine, stirring until dissolved. Mix with the ground tongue and eggs. Add Worcestershire and more salt to taste. Turn into a mould. Set in ice box to harden. Serve on a platter of lettuce leaves or grape leaves, and pass a generous bowl of tart mayonnaise.

Individual Creamed Chicken Salad

Proportions for each individual salad, to be increased to desired quantity.

⅛ teaspoon gelatine soaked in
¾ teaspoon lemon juice and dissolved in
1 teaspoon boiling water
1½ teaspoons heavy cream beaten until stiff, to which is added
the gelatine mixture
Set in ice box
When mixture begins to thicken, add
3 tablespoons cold cooked chicken cut in cubes, preferably white
meat, mixed with
¼ tablespoon chopped parsley
Salt to taste

Put into an individual mould shaken out of cold water. Place in ice box to harden. Serve on a crisp lettuce leaf and garnish with a sprig of parsley.

Idella's Cheese Souffle

1 cup rich milk
2 tablespoons flour
2 tablespoons butter
¼ tablespoon salt
1 packed cup grated cheese
3 eggs

Make a cream sauce of the butter, flour, milk and salt. While hot, stir in the grated cheese. Add one unbeaten egg yolk at a time to the mixture, stirring well, beating between eggs. Fold in the egg whites beaten until stiff. Pour into buttered casserole, and set the casserole in a pan containing one and one-half inches of cold water. Bake forty-five minutes at a temperature of three hundred and fifty degrees. This soufflé holds up without falling better than any I know, but even so, it is advisable to serve it instantly. Serves four to six.

Salmon Loaf

    1 can salmon
    1 pint milk
    2 tablespoons butter
    3 tablespoons flour
    1 tablespoon chopped parsley
    4 hard-boiled egg yolks
    Salt and pepper to taste

Make a cream sauce of the butter, flour and milk and one-half teaspoon salt and a dash of pepper. Add the salmon, broken into flakes lightly, the hard-boiled egg yolks broken fine with a fork, and more salt if desired. Turn into a buttered baking dish, brush with beaten egg, cover with bread crumbs, dot with butter, and bake quickly. Serves four.

Rum Omelet

4 eggs
½ cup cream sauce
1 cup mixed fruits
½ cup rum
Serves 2 to 3

Cool the cream sauce until lukewarm and add to the well beaten egg yolks, mixing well. Beat the egg whites until stiff and fold in. Pour into a deep iron skillet in which has been melted one tablespoon butter. Cook over a moderate flame. Shake the pan gently occasionally until omelet thickens and puffs and browns lightly on the under side. Place in a hot oven for a few minutes until omelet is thoroughly puffed and set. Remove from oven. Cut slightly down the middle. Have ready a very hot platter. Turn the mixed fruit on one side of the omelet, fold over the other side, and turn out quickly onto platter. Sprinkle top of omelet with granulated sugar. Pour over the rum. Set ablaze. Have ready a long-handled spoon and a long-tined toasting fork. As rum blazes, prick omelet through here and there and ladle up the blazing rum from the sides of the tilted platter and baste the omelet. This is done at the table. Cut in portions and serve just as the flame dies down.

The rum should be either the one hundred and fifty proof strong rum, or two tablespoons pure grain alcohol should be added to ordinary rum, to insure a good blaze.

The most satisfactory fruit is the commercial canned "fruit cocktail." To three-quarters cup of this is added one small can of canned figs, or the same amount of fresh cooked sugar figs. For my own mixture, I use a combination of canned pineapple diced small, tangerines cut small, canned pears diced small, canned peaches diced small, canned seedless grapes, and above all, the figs. The figs and pineapple are the most important of the fruits.

Pecan Patties

1 cup coarse bread crumbs
2 tablespoons finely minced onion
⅛ teaspoon salt
4 tablespoons milk
1 egg
⅓ cup finely broken or cut pecans

Mix bread crumbs, onion, salt, milk and slightly beaten egg and let stand half an hour. Stir in the finely broken pecan meats and shape into small patties. Fry in hot butter, turning once, until a brown crust forms on both sides. Serve at once.

Vegetables

Charles Browne, in his delightful *Gun Club Cook Book*, remarks that "brocoli may be spelled with two c's, but that does not help its flavor." Great gourmet that he is, he has obviously never had broccoli fresh from his own garden. A few vegetables survive time, tide and transportation. Most of them lose so much with every hour after their picking, that sometimes, as with broccoli, the store-bought variety bears no recognizable relation to the fresh garden variety. Corn on the cob and green peas also suffer, past belief, a loss of flavor. My grandmother would not allow green corn to be broken from the stalks until dinner was almost ready for serving. I should not dream of cutting my broccoli earlier than an hour before meal-time. When a garden is not at hand, or a neighboring farmer, the quick-frozen vegetables are to be preferred to most vegetables more than twelve hours from their time and place of picking.

Most cooks nowadays understand the cooking of vegetables, knowing that the use of the least possible water is important, and the serving of the juices along with the vegetable when practicable. Both vitamins and flavor are so retained. Beautiful bright-green vegetables may be obtained by boiling with a pinch of soda and in a larger quantity of water that is drained off before serving, but this is a sacrifice of health that should be indulged in only in serving a decorator's meal or in showing off. Butter should not be spared in dressing plain vegetables. Without enough of it, vegetables betray themselves too painfully as roots and herbs. A cream sauce, or thin cream and butter, is often a delightful addition to carrots, lima beans, cauliflower, kohl-rabi and the like, but it is kind only to serve it to the thin. Cream sauce au gratin makes a main luncheon dish of spinach, chayotes, broccoli, kohl-rabi, asparagus, cauliflower or onions. I am an addict of Hollandaise sauce and it is my choice for lifting broccoli, asparagus, okra, and cauliflower in particular, to dizzy heights of edibility. Unless the Hollandaise is perfection, butter and lemon are a safer dressing. I give here only the vegetables that are a *spécialité du maison* at Cross Creek.

Broccoli A la Hollandaise

Cut broccoli heads or flowerets an hour before meal-time. Discard any portion of the stalk with a tendency to toughness. Wash and let stand in cold water. Have ready boiling, slightly salted water that will no more than cover the broccoli. Boil twenty minutes. Drain well, cover with Hollandaise sauce and serve at once. To make sure that the temperamental Hollandaise and the broccoli are ready at the same time, I make the Hollandaise in the top of a glass double boiler five minutes before the broccoli is done. The Hollandaise can safely be set off the fire while the broccoli is draining in a colander—no longer.

Hollandaise Sauce

Measurements for individual serving.

¼ cup butter
Yolk of 1 egg
Juice of ½ lemon
⅛ teaspoon salt

Increase according to number to be served.

Divide butter in three pieces. Put one piece in the top of a double boiler over boiling water with the egg yolks and lemon juice. Do not allow the boiling water quite to reach the bottom of the top of the double boiler. Stir rapidly and constantly. As butter melts, add another third-portion. When mixture begins to thicken, add the third piece and the salt. As soon as thickened, SNATCH from the fire. The tricks in successful Hollandaise are constant stirring; not cooking one second too long; and being ready to serve it the moment it is taken from the fire.

Okra A la Cross Creek

Have ready boiling, lightly salted water. Choose only tiny very young fresh okra pods. Wash. Do not cut off the stem end, as you trust me. Drop whole pods in rapidly boiling water and boil exactly seven minutes from the time the water resumes its boiling. Not a moment longer. Drain quickly. Arrange like the spokes of a wheel on hot individual serving dishes. Place individual bowls of Hollandaise in the centers of the dishes. The okra is eaten as one eats unhulled strawberries, lifting with the fingers by the stem end and dipping into the Hollandaise. I recommend this to those who think they don't like okra. It is firm, not slimy, and with the sauce, superb. I usually serve twelve okra pods per person.

Beets in Orange Juice

Use either freshly cooked beets or canned beets. Slice thin and heat, without boiling, in one-half cup orange juice, one tablespoon butter and grated rind of one orange, to every two cups of sliced beets, which will serve six.

Beets with Orange Sauce

Use shoestring beets or tiny whole beets
Serve with orange sauce
1 cup orange juice
⅓ cup sugar
2 tablespoons cornstarch
1 tablespoon butter
⅛ teaspoon salt

Combine sugar, salt and cornstarch, mixing well. Add orange juice and butter and cook five minutes or until thick in top of double boiler.

Here again, the sauce transmutes the common beet into a dish one eats for pleasure, not for duty.

Carrots Glazed in Honey

Boil whole small carrots until tender but still firm. Use a small enough amount of water so that it boils entirely away. To every bunch of carrots—about six or eight—allow two or three tablespoons butter and one-third cup strained honey. Add butter and honey to cooked, dry carrots and simmer slowly until carrots are glazed and brown, turning once or twice. Allow two or three small carrots per person.

Carrot Souffle

> 2 cups cooked carrots
> 1 teaspoon salt
> ¼ cup strained honey
> 1¼ cups very rich milk or thin cream
> 3 tablespoons cornstarch
> 3 eggs
> 4 tablespoons melted butter
> Serves 6 to 8

Put the cooked carrots through a sieve. Stir in the salt and honey, the milk, in which has been dissolved the cornstarch, then add the well beaten eggs, and last, the melted butter. Pour into a buttered casserole and bake forty-five minutes in a four-hundred-degree oven. People like this who usually turn up their noses at carrots.

As far as I know, this is my own concoction. It tastes almost too good to be true.

Braised Onions (Marvelous with Duck or Goose

Peel medium to small white onions and cook them whole in a small quantity of lightly salted water. I allow four small onions or two or three medium ones per person. Cook until extremely tender, allowing all the water to boil away. Add one tablespoon butter and one teaspoon sugar for every four to six onions, according to size. Simmer gently until onions are well browned all over, turning often. Serve with the brown juice.

Corn Souffle

1 can corn or
2 cups cooked corn cut from the cob
1 teaspoon salt
1 tablespoon sugar
2 cups very rich milk
1 tablespoon cornstarch
3 or 4 eggs
4 tablespoons melted butter
Serves 6

Put the corn through a sieve. Add the salt, sugar and milk, in which has been dissolved the cornstarch. Add the well-beaten eggs, then the melted butter. Turn into a buttered casserole and bake forty-five minutes in a four-hundred-degree oven. This is very good as a vegetable with ham or pork or chicken.

The chayote is distinctly a tropical vegetable. I grieve to speak of it to those who may live their lives without tasting it. It is a member of the squash family and grows on a handsome green vine that has been known to cover an acre. Through one hot summer I trained a vine from my garden over the Mallards' duck-pen, so that it provided shade for them. The chayotes grow pendulous, pear-shaped, their color the palest jade-green. They can be eaten at almost any stage of their development. The flavor resembles faintly that of kohl-rabi, but is much more delicate. The texture is fine and pear-like. Since they keep a very long time and ship easily, it is possible that they may eventually reach markets far from their home.

I peel them, and if the large single central seed is still embryonic, leave it as part of the dish. The chayote may be cut in sizeable cubes or straight across in half-inch slices, boiled in a little water, salted, and served with melted butter or with Hollandaise. It is good served in a thin cream sauce. It is best au gratin.

Chayotes Au Gratin

Prepare as above, boil twenty minutes or until tender but not mushy, drain. Place in a buttered baking dish, cover with a rather thick cream sauce, top with a thick layer of grated or finely cut cheese. Bake until cheese is well-browned. Muffins make an ideal accompaniment. With a tart jelly or citrus marmalade, and a salad, it makes a complete luncheon or light supper dish, like any vegetable suitable for serving au gratin.

Poke weed was "relished" by our pioneer forbears, both for its flavor and as a source of "greens" in the springtime. Since it grows, I believe, over most of the country, I recommend it to any table. "Poke salat" in the south may be the new green leaves either cut up and dressed with salt and pepper and vinegar, or boiled with white bacon (salt pork). My favorite method of serving it is as a substitute for asparagus. In the spring I watch after every rain for the slender pale green shoots. I cut only the young, tender ones not more than six or eight inches in height.

Poke Weed Cross Creek

Strip the leaves and skin from the shoots. Wash well. Boil whole for fifteen minutes or until tender in salted water. Drain. Place on toast and cover with a rich cream sauce. Serve with crisp breakfast bacon and with a tart jelly if desired. This too makes a complete meal and has a delightful flavor, with a slight taste of iron. I imagine that the dish is rich in minerals.

Collard Greens

Wash collard leaves. They should not be too old and coarse. Cut finely. Boil until extremely tender, a matter of at least an hour, preferably longer—they can scarcely be cooked too long, and are equally good "warmed over"—in enough water barely to cover, with several thin slices of white bacon to each market bunch of the leaves. The water should almost cook away, leaving a cup or two of a delicious broth known to the South as "pot liquor." Cornbread is always served with collard greens and it is etiquette to dunk the cornbread in the pot liquor.

Collard greens and cornbread are a mark of the plain people, and Southern politicians make a point of their passion for them in their campaign speeches. Their stigma as a dish for the humble cost me the only elegant servant I ever had at Cross Creek. His name was Godfrey, and he came first to the farmhouse to give a touch of swank to a buffet supper that I served a group of male intelligentsia who paid me the compliment of coming to me once a year for their meeting, at which an erudite paper was read. Like Mother's Embroidery Club, they had an eye to the table, and I did my culinary best. I drove to Ocala for Godfrey on the day of the party, brought him home to the Creek, and gave him detailed instructions as to the portions of the supper that I wished him to prepare. He was a tall, handsome, elderly, light brown Negro who gave an air to any function. As time proved, an air was all that Godfrey contributed. After some two hours, when I had busied myself in the front of the house with flower arranging and so forth, I went back to the kitchen. I had no household help at the time except an occasional filling-in by the faithful Negress Martha, who had all the good will in the world, but scarcely knew a fork from a spoon. There was a field-hand to assist her in dishwashing. Godfrey was standing at the long pine kitchen table slicing kumquats wafer-thin, while Martha and the field-hand stood lost in utter idleness and admiration, watching him. As far as I could determine, he had been doing nothing but slicing kumquats. I pitched in and did all the things he was supposed to have done, set him at arranging his table for the serving of drinks, and by a miracle was ready for my guests when they arrived.

The paper was on the abstruse subject of Cosmology. Afterward there was deep discussion. After supper, Godfrey hovered in the background for the serving of drinks and the lighting of cigars and cigarettes. When I took him back to Ocala that night, he thanked me for the privilege of serving such brilliant minds.

"The gentleman who gave the paper," he said, "really knew his astronomy."

Then, "I understand the position in your household is open. I should like to join your establishment."

The *job* was open, I mentioned the not-too-high wages I could afford to pay, and said, "You realize, you would be expected to do almost everything, except the washing and ironing."

Godfrey accepted, and deciding that his age and dignity would preclude criticism from Cross Creek on my having a man-servant, I brought him out, bag and baggage, to the vacant tenant house on the grove. Too late, it appeared that not only had Godfrey never boiled an egg nor made a pot of coffee, but that he had believed that Martha and the field-hand were permanent servants, and all he would have to do would be a bit of light dusting, and the serving of extraordinary meals and drinks to a constant procession of guests who talked of Cosmology. Godfrey was floored and so was I. I think we were both very sporting about it. He condescended to learn to make my breakfast coffee, to do housecleaning, while I did the major part of the cooking.

Relations became strained when he placed one of his favorite books on every breakfast tray. My early hours with my coffee are my only assured moments of peace at the Creek, and I did not propose to spend them reading *Early Christian Martyrs*. Relations came to an impasse the day I ordered collard greens and cornbread for my lunch. Godfrey murmured polite protests, already grieved that I had not repeated daily the buffet supper of jellied fruit cup, ham baked in sherry, roast wild duck, sweet potato baskets and so forth. But collard greens and cornbread were what I wanted, and I started him off firmly on their preparation.

Ritual was necessary for Godfrey and when I had seen the cooking through and lunch was ready, he came to the veranda, drew out my chair for me with formality, and brought back the collard greens and cornbread in my best silver serving dishes, his nose in the air. At that moment I observed that a neighbor's cows had broken through the fence and were browsing on my orange trees.

I shrieked, "Godfrey, the cows! The cows!" and ran to drive them out.

Godfrey followed at a broken-hearted distance and gave notice. He grieved at leaving me, he declared, but the establishment had not proved what he expected.

He said mournfully, "I should like to serve you. You are a wonderful woman."

Remembering my patience, I murmured, "You're telling me?" and took him back to Ocala.

A friend reported passing him on the street, unemployed, he happened to know, and saying to his companion, "As Tennyson says——"

French Fried Eggplant

Peel an egg-plant and cut lengthwise in finger-size strips. Soak one hour in cold salted water. Drain, soak in plain cold water one-half hour, drain again and dry well. Sprinkle lightly with salt and pepper, dip in flour, then in slightly beaten egg, then in bread crumbs, and fry until a rich brown in deep smoking fat. One medium-sized eggplant serves four to six.

Fried Asparagus

Large-sized canned asparagus is good fried this way, with no preliminary preparation other than draining and light salting and peppering. Yellow summer squash is good, too, but cut crosswise in quarter-inch slices.

Parsnip Croquettes

Folk who would rather starve than eat parsnips would make a sizeable army. Charles Browne describes parsnips as tasting like gun-powder. There is little excuse for eating plain boiled parsnips, and fried parsnips are none too tempting, but parsnip croquettes are the ugly duckling become a swan.

Boil whole unpeeled parsnips, in slightly salted boiling water until very tender. Plunge in cold water and remove the skins and the core. Mash. To each cup, add one-half teaspoon salt, one tablespoon sugar, one beaten egg and a dash of grated nutmeg. Shape into small croquettes, roll in flour, and fry either in deep hot fat or in butter in a skillet. One cup of mashed parsnips, made into croquettes, serves three.

Cow-Peas

Cow-peas are a summer staple in the South. They are served, with apologies, on city tables, without apology on country tables, and greeted with gusto at both. We have black-eyed peas, little white conch peas (perhaps the best) and whippoor-will. I am sometimes guilty of planting my sixteen-acre hay-field to whippoorwill instead of ordinary field peas, so that the colored folks may have their fill, even though the resulting cow-pea hay is not so desirable. As with collard greens, we cook cow-peas with white bacon and serve them with cornbread. The cow-peas and bacon are simply boiled together in water to cover until both are tender. Rural Florida folk cook green peas, which we call English peas, and fresh lima beans, which we call Fordhooks, with white bacon, but here I part company with the rest of the Creek. Nothing but Dora's butter, with perhaps a little of her cream, is delicate enough for their pale sweet taste.

Hopping John

1 cup cow-peas
¼ lb. white bacon
½ cup rice
3 cups water
Salt to taste
Serves 4

Boil together cow-peas and bacon cut in slices in three cups water, adding one-half teaspoon salt. When tender, add the separately cooked fluffy rice. Cook a few minutes more. Serve with cornbread. A small onion is sometimes diced and cooked with the peas.

Chinese Cabbage, Cross Creek

In the bottom of a kettle place one finely chopped onion and three strips of breakfast bacon cut in small pieces. Brown together. Slice thinly one stalk of Chinese cabbage, crosswise, soak in cold water, and dip from the pan of water directly into the kettle, allowing as much water as possible to adhere to the cabbage. No more water is needed if the kettle is very tightly covered. Simmer gently thirty minutes, or until the cabbage is tender and the moisture has cooked away. The browned bacon bits and onion give flavor to the cabbage, otherwise rather insipid when cooked. One Chinese cabbage serves three.

Swamp Cabbage
(Hearts of Palm)

I always feel a little uneasy in recommending swamp cabbage (hearts of palm at the Ritz), for this greatest of Florida vegetables is the white core of a young palm tree, and its cutting means the death of the tree. I fear always that some enterprising backwoodsman will take a notion to send them to market, and that the beautiful tropical palm groves will be decimated. Swamp cabbage is the sportsman's friend, for he can usually manage to make camp near a palm grove, and take his vegetable to accompany his fish or game directly from the land. Most of us are honorable, do not take more than we need, and try to choose a young tree from a clump from which it will not be missed. The tree must be no more than eight or ten feet in height, or the core will be tough and bitter. Palms growing too close to water are also likely to be bitter. The Florida bears know the goodness of this food, and in the bear region west of the St. Johns River, we find palms slashed to their roots by sharp claws and the hearts torn out as though by giant forks.

Swamp Cabbage Salad

Only an expert can cut down a palm and strip the core properly to its ivory-white, layered heart. The lower portion of the heart must be tested by taste for bitterness, the upper portion, for fibrousness, until one is down to a white cylinder of complete sweetness and tender crispness. Slice thinly and soak for an hour in ice water. Drain well, serve with French dressing or a tart mayonnaise. The flavor is much like chestnuts.

Swamp Cabbage, Camp Style

Prepare swamp cabbage as above. Boil slowly in as little water as possible, with several slices of white bacon. The bacon will probably provide sufficient salt. Pepper may be added if desired. If palm heart has any tendency to bitterness, parboil for five minutes, drain off water, and cover with fresh boiling water. Otherwise cook, tightly covered, for forty-five minutes or until meltingly tender, and until most of the moisture has been absorbed.

Swamp Cabbage, Cross Creek

Instead of white bacon, add two tablespoons of Dora's butter and a half teaspoon of salt to sliced palm heart and cook in very little water until dry and thoroughly tender. Add one-half to one cup of Dora's cream, heated, quantity according to amount of palm heart. Heat to simmering and serve at once. Prepared this way, heart of palm is fit for a king.

Potatoes, Rice and Grits
Baked Stuffed Potatoes

Bake large baking potatoes, preferably Idaho or Vermont bakers. Slice off the top to the depth of one-half inch. Scoop out potatoes into bowl, mash well, beat in rich milk until consistency of heavy mashed potatoes, salt, pepper, one egg and four teaspoons butter to every four potatoes. Pile, leaving a rough, peaked surface, into baked shells. Brush over with milk. Brown in hot oven. These may be prepared in advance of a meal, and brushed with milk and browned when ready to serve, allowing a longer time in such a case for thorough heating through. Garnish with a sprig of parsley in every potato.

Scalloped Potatoes

Fill a baking dish with layers of sliced raw potatoes. Dot every layer with generous dots of butter, salt, pepper, and a dusting of flour. Pour over rich milk to cover. Bake in a moderate oven until tender and well browned on top. This method gives a flavor superior to previously cooked potatoes scalloped.

A light layer of grated cheese to every layer of potatoes, and a more generous layer on top, give a delicious potatoes au gratin.

Potato Croquettes

1 cup seasoned mash potatoes,
    hot or cold
1 tablespoon onion juice
1 teaspoon minced parsley
1 egg, stirred in

Mould into balls a little smaller than a golf ball, or into small cylinders. Chill thoroughly. Dip in beaten egg, then roll in fine bread crumbs, and fry in deep hot fat. These make a "company" dish at any time, or help to dress up a meal of cold meats. Serves four.

Sweet Potato Croquettes

1 cup boiled, mashed sweet potatoes
Salt to taste
2 tablespoons heavy cream
1 egg, stirred in

Chill. Form into small cylinders. Chill again. Dip in beaten egg, then in fine bread crumbs. Fry in deep hot fat. These are especially good served with ham or pork, poultry or game. For serving with ham, a dash of clove, a grating of nutmeg, one-eighth teaspoon powdered cinnamon and one teaspoon of brown sugar, added to the mixture, give a piquancy to the croquettes. Serves four.

Candied Sweet Potatoes

Boil medium-sized sweet potatoes until tender, but not soft. Allow one potato per person. Drain and cool. Peel. Slice lengthwise in halves, or to a thickness of one-third inch. Butter well a shallow baking pan. Place sliced potatoes flat. Barely cover with an uncooked syrup made of brown sugar and water, allowing about one cup of the sweetening to one-half cup water. Or use straight maple syrup or honey. Dot generously with butter. Bake slowly until most of syrup has been absorbed, turning once, until potatoes are browned and well glazed. These are especially delicious with baked ham.

Sweet Potato Souffle

> 2 cups boiled, mashed sweet potatoes
> ¾ teaspoon salt
> 2 cups rich milk or thin cream
> ½ cup honey
> 2 tablespoons cornstarch, dissolved in
>   4 tablespoons of the milk or cream
> 3 beaten eggs
> 1 cup broken pecan meats
> Marshmallows
> Serves 6 to 8

Blend all ingredients except marshmallows, in order. Place in deep buttered casserole or baking dish. Bake slowly thirty to forty minutes, or until set, so that silver knife thrust into soufflé comes out clean. Cover top with marshmallows. Continue baking until marshmallows are puffed and brown. Serve immediately. This is one of the most luscious and utterly deadly dishes that I serve. I constantly expect guests to fall in convulsions after partaking.

It is possible to omit the marshmallows, dotting with butter instead, and/or the pecans, but one might as well go the whole hog.

Sweet Potato Apple Souffle

Make soufflé as above, using one-quarter cup honey or one-quarter cup brown sugar instead of one-half cup honey. Omit pecans. Place potato mixture in layers in baking dish, alternating with layers of quartered or sliced apples. Clove and cinnamon, to taste, may be added if desired. Marshmallows, at the end, or dots of butter, on the top. Longer cooking is necessary because of the apples.

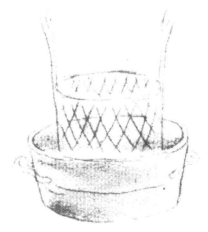

Grits

Grits are the Deep South member of the hominy family. Wha
the North knows as hominy, we call "big hominy." This is the
whole grains of white corn treated, amazingly, with lye, and
boiled. Grits are hominy dried and ground fine. They are a
staple food in Florida, backwoodsmen eating them three time:
a day and considering a day without grits, a day wasted. A taste
for grits must be cultivated by outsiders, and in any Southern
eating place, Yankee tourists may be recognized by their re
action to grits, especially at breakfast. We use them in place o
potatoes. Never as a cereal. For the benefit of Northern cooks
they may be found in many grocery stores, packaged, and la
beled "Hominy Grits." These are coarser than Southern grits

> 1 cup grits, washed
> 4 cups boiling water
> 1 teaspoon salt
> Serves 3 to 4

Stir the grits slowly into the boiling water. Cover and let cook
slowly, about thirty to forty minutes, stirring often. There are
addicts of "soft grits" for whom more hot water must be added
to the cooking mixture. Most of us prefer them of the consist
ency of mush.

Florida country folk use grits as a base for "gravy." The
gravy, unhappily, consists only of the grease from any fat meat
usually that of white bacon (fat salt pork). Rural gravy i
one spot where I part company with my neighbors. Grits with
butter are a necessity with fried fish. The combination is "a

natural." Grits are good served with scrambled eggs, or with a poached egg on top of each serving. A Cross Creek friend horrified me by calling for grits to which he added chopped raw onion and sardines. I tasted dubiously, and remained to gorge.

Cheese Grits

Cheese grits seem to be a Baskin (Alabama) specialty. They are a major contribution to good Southern eating. To one kettle of grits, as above, stir in, when done, one cup medium strong shaved cheese. Blend well, and let cook a few minutes. As a breakfast dish, with scrambled eggs, bacon and crisp biscuits, I know no greater feast.

Fried Cheese Grits

Pack left-over cheese grits in a square or rectangular pan. Chill in ice box. Cut in slices three or four inches long and one inch in width. Dip in beaten egg, then in flour. Fry on both sides in butter until well browned. Plain grits are also chilled and fried in this way, and are superb with duck, ham, any game—or with almost anything.

Cheese Grits Souffle

Blend
½ of cheese grits recipe, cold
¾ teaspoon salt
1 cup milk, blending well
3 well-beaten eggs
Serves 4

Mix, in order of ingredients, beating until smooth. Turn into buttered baking dish. Bake at three hundred and seventy-five degrees for forty-five minutes. Four to six servings, according to capacity. This is wonderful.

Fluffy Rice

1 cup washed rice
1 teaspoon salt
Deep kettle of boiling water,
**   at least 3 quarts**

Add rice slowly to boiling salted water. Partially cover. Boil briskly about twenty minutes, or until rice is very tender. Drain into colander. Pour fresh boiling water over and set, covered, over hot water for about ten minutes. Each grain stands out dry and separate. Serves four.

Wild rice should be cooked in this way. Wild rice swells greatly, and less is needed, one-half cup serving four.

Rice Croquettes

¾ cup uncooked rice
1½ cups boiling water
1 teaspoon salt
1½ cups scalding milk
2 tablespoons butter
2 tablespoons sugar
Yolks of 3 eggs
Serves 6

Put rice, water, butter and salt in the top of a double boiler and cook over boiling water until perfectly dry. With a fork, stir in the hot milk. Cook until milk is absorbed. Add well beaten egg yolks, then sugar, stirring all through the rice with a fork. Turn into a shallow pan to cool and chill thoroughly in the ice box. Form into round balls about one and one-half inches in diameter and make a small depression in each. Chill again. Dip in beaten egg, then in fine cracker crumbs or fine bread crumbs and fry in a basket in deep hot fat until a rich brown. Serve at once. Place a generous cube of very tart jelly—currant, wild grape or wild plum—in the slight depression in each croquette.

Sweet Potatoes in Orange Baskets

1 cup mashed boiled sweet potatoes
⅛ teaspoon salt
1 tablespoon honey
2 tablespoons cream
1 egg, stirred in
Dash of clove
Grated rind of 1 orange

Cut oranges in half and scoop out pulp, saving for salad or fruit cup or a dessert. Fill shells with potato mixture. Place a half-teaspoon of butter on top of each. Bake in a hot oven until faintly browned. Handles may be made of orange rind if one wants to be very fancy.

Souffle Potatoes

Slice raw white potatoes thin and evenly. Chill in ice water. Drain well between towels. Fry about eight minutes in deep fat that is not very hot. Drain and chill in ice box. Plunge, not too many at a time, in smoking hot fat and fry quickly. Drain, salt and serve. They are supposed to puff up, crisp on the outside, hollow inside. They do puff up at the famous Antoine's, in New Orleans. In the home kitchen, for some mysterious reason, they are not so spectacular.

Florida Sea Foods

Behind Florida sea foods are all the beauty and excitement of lake and river and the great sea itself. The little shrimp boats bob like tops in front of my summer cottage on the ocean. Their nets, larger than the boats themselves, bring in to the St. Augustine wholesale markets the jumbo shrimp that fry to such a nutty delectability. A man wades barelegged at low tide in the salt Matanzas River. He throws, with incredible grace, his cast net, and brings in the small, sweet river shrimp so fine for cocktails or pilau.

The markets are piled with deep-sea fish, still alive when the fishermen empty their baskets into the great scales—pompano, the aristocrat of ocean fishes, Spanish mackerel, bluefish, mullet, red snapper, sea-trout, king mackerel and whiting. Flounders are there, too, but when possible we like to hunt our own. It is truly hunting rather than fishing, for we walk at night just on the turn of the incoming tide through the sloughs and inlets of small bays of the ocean, or at the edge of the surf. One holds a lantern and the others carry gigs. A shadow stirs, or a quick eye spots a triangular mound of sand in the shallow water, the gig darts, and another flounder is added to the sack. Flounder is served at the best hotels as filet of sole, and some consider it even superior to the true Dover sole. The meat is white, sweet and flaky and is best when broiled.

I am in disgrace at present over the matter of flounders. Idella and I came to my ocean cottage south of St. Augustine in a recent heat wave. I walked out on the beach early one morning and found that the tide had left a deep slough, cut off from the main body of the ocean. On the bottom of the slough were slowly swimming two flounders. It had been three years since I had night-hunted them with friends and I was delighted. I had nothing with which to catch them but my bare hands, but surely that would do, since the flounders could not, eventually, escape. I made a grab for the largest and received such an electric shock that I was hurled to the sand. Nobody had told me flounders were dangerous. I remembered that rubber was an insulator against electricity, removed my bathing cap, cupped it around one hand, and scooped patiently and persistently under each flounder in turn until inch by inch I had flipped them out onto the sand. I carried them home triumphantly by the tails, insulated by the cap, Idella rejoiced with me, and we had fried flounder and grits for lunch.

The next day I watched the tide and set out again when the same condition of the slough was visible. This time there were three flounders paddling about. I was armed now with a wooden-handled long toasting fork, and I speared my quarry with this, going waist-deep after the last one. No hunter from the hills ever went home, prouder of his good providing, than I. I felt that Idella and I could make out on a desert island. This morning it happened that an old fisherman was doing a bit of grass-cutting for me. Idella was busy and I suggested that Leyton clean my catch. Idella took him fish, knife and pan.

"What's that?" He is very deaf and Idella shouted.

"That's flounder."

"No, God," Leyton shouted back.

My "flounders" were electric rays. No self-respecting starving dog has ever been known to eat them——

The best fish in the world are of course those one catches oneself. Aside from the satisfaction to the ego, they are better simply because they are fresh. Every hour that fish is out of the water is flavor lost. Shell cracker bream from Shands canal are better at Cross Creek, perch from Orange Lake, than pompano that must be transported from the coast. Friends who eat frog-legs at the Creek swear they have never had such frog-legs before. I take no credit for my cooking of them. It is only that they have come the night before from the Orange Lake marshes behind my farmhouse, and all the goodness is still in them.

Frog-hunting is the livelihood of half the inhabitants of the Creek. The market price is high, and a Creek frog-hunter may make enough in one night's hunting, with small poled boat, flashlight and gig, to idle to his taste the rest of the week. I must pay fifty cents a pound for the dressed legs, and even then am doing the hunter no commercial favor.

If I had to choose one dish on which to claim laurels as a cook, I think it might be my Crab à la Newburg. Again, the honors should go to Dora, my Jersey cow, and to the crab-meat. There are two deep springs in the heart of the Big Scrub that are the source of blue crabs so large, so sweet, that I shudder selfishly lest some day the world should discover them. We drive some fifty miles from Cross Creek into the Scrub, to where the springs appear mysteriously from nowhere, to form lovely small jungle streams. They join, eventually, the ocean, and are teeming with enormous blue ocean crabs, the meat somehow sweeter and more tender from the slightly mineral waters. We hunt them by night, drifting slowly downstream in a rowboat with flashlight and long handled crab-claws that clamp shut when they strike the crab, spotted through the deep clear water by our light. We take no more than we shall use. For eating just-so, boiled and served cold with mayonnaise, French or Cuban bread and cold ale, we catch three crabs per person. For making crab salad, stuffed crab or crab à la Newburg, two crabs per person are sufficient. The crabs are plunged alive in boiling well-salted water. Back at the Creek kitchen, sensing their doom as the kettle boils, they have a trick of escaping from the crocus sack over the kitchen floor. It has sometimes taken my dog, my cat and several guests to help me, perilously, round them up again. They are boiled twenty minutes, dropped briefly in cold water, the shells, small claws and dead-man's fingers discarded, and the flavorsome huge morsels picked out by hand to be prepared according to one's ability and eaten according to one's capacity.

Crab A la Newburg, Cross Creek

2 heaping cupfuls of crab meat
½ cup of Dora's butter
2 cupfuls of cream
2 tablespoons flour
Juice of 1 lemon
4 eggs
¾ teaspoon salt
Pepper
Dash of clove
½ teaspoon paprika
½ cup dry sherry
1 tablespoon brandy
Serves 4 to 6 according to appetite

Melt the butter in an iron skillet but do not brown. Stir in the crab meat gently. Sauté for one minute. Add lemon juice. Stir in flour. Add cream slowly, stirring constantly and lightly. When sauce is smooth, add salt, pepper, clove and paprika and let mixture bubble five minutes. Have ready the piping hot serving dish, hot plates and toast points. Warn the guests to drink their last cocktail or highball. Stir in the sherry. Beat the eggs just short of foaminess and stir in quickly. Add the brandy. Rush the Newburg, garnished with parsley, and the guests, instantly to table. Serve with any dry white wine and any green salad made with French dressing. Sit back and await compliments.

In pity for folk who do not own a Dora, I must admit that city cream is useable, less butter possible, and two eggs may be used instead of four, substituting another tablespoon of flour. The brandy may be omitted, but never the sherry.

Crab Salad

2 cups crab meat
½ cup diced cucumber
¼ cup finely cut celery
½ cup home-made mayonnaise, made with
    lemon juice
Serves 4 to 6

Serve on crisp lettuce leaves, with extra bowl of mayonnaise. Any decoration is a desecration. Serve thin bread and butter sandwiches or cream-cheese sandwiches.

Deviled Crab

To recipe for stuffed crab, add one teaspoon dry mustard, one green pepper and one pimiento finely cut.

Stuffed Crab

4 cups crab meat
1 cup milk
3 thick slices of white bread, crusts removed
¼ lb. Dora's butter
3 large tablespoons chopped parsley
1½ large tablespoons grated onion
¾ teaspoon salt (or to taste), dash of pepper
Dash of Tabasco or Datil pepper sauce
3 tablespoons Worcestershire sauce

Cook all ingredients except crab meat ten minutes, stirring. Add crab meat. Cook five minutes. Fill crab shells. This recipe fills six. Sprinkle bread crumbs over top, and brown in hot oven. Datil pepper sauce may be had only in St. Augustine, and a trip for the purpose is almost worth while. The Datil pepper is a small lean yellow-green pepper, Spanish or Minorcan in origin, very hot and of a distinct pungency. The sauce is made by filling a bottle with the whole peppers and covering with vinegar or sherry.

Buttered Crabs

Boil whole crabs twenty minutes in salted water. Remove shells, small claws, and dead-man's fingers. Melt one-half pound Dora's butter in a deep pan. Drop in crab bodies. Cover tightly and steam for one-half hour. Place on platter with the large claws. Every man is on his own.

Sautéd Crab Meat

2 cups crab meat
4 tablespoons Dora's butter
¼ teaspoon salt (or to taste)
Dash of pepper, dash of paprika

Cook crab meat in butter and seasonings five minutes. Serve on buttered toast, or fold into an omelet. Serves four to six.

Crab Patties

2 cups crab meat
1 cup bread crumbs
½ cup milk
2 eggs, beaten
2 tablespoons chopped parsley
1 tablespoon Worcestershire sauce
½ teaspoon salt

Mix well, form into small patties, fry in butter. Serve with lemon butter or Tartar sauce. Serves four to six.

Crab Souffle

2 cups crab meat
1 cup rich cream sauce
3 eggs, well beaten
1 tablespoon chopped parsley

Place in buttered baking dish, cover with bread crumbs and dots of butter. Bake slowly until brown. Serves four to six.

Crab Meat au Gratin

2 cups crab meat
1 cup rich cream sauce
½ cup grated cheese

Blend crab meat and cream sauce. Place in buttered baking dish. Cover with grated cheese. Bake in hot oven until brown. Serves four to six.

Fresh-caught shrimp have spoiled those of us with access to Florida's coasts for the canned variety. There is no comparison in either flavor or texture. We prefer to be waiting at the St. Augustine fish markets when the day's catch is brought in from the shrimp boats, and to go off with a sack of beheaded shrimp that were wriggling an hour ago. We plunge the shrimp in boiling well-salted water—some like a teaspoon of cayenne pepper in the water, too—and boil them briskly for twenty minutes, until the shrimp are a rich pink in color. I myself drain them and turn cold water on them for just a minute, then drain again. This seems to set the flesh in a firm tenderness. Place in ice box to chill. When ready to use, peel off the shells and remove the black line down the backs. For deep-fried shrimp, leave the tail intact in its shell. The tail makes a fine "lifter" for holding the shrimp, which should be eaten from the fingers. The tip also fries to a brown crispness that many find delicious.

St. Augustine
Deep-Fried Sea Shrimp

Peel large fresh uncooked shrimp, leaving the tail on. Remove

the dark line down the back, split down the back without
separating, wash, press flat, season with salt, roll in flour, dip in
beaten egg, then in fine cracker meal or bread crumbs. Fry
until a rich brown in deep smoking fat. Serve with tartar sauce
and garnish with lemon segments and parsley. Serve six to eight
jumbo shrimps per person.

Shrimp Newburg

Follow recipe for Crab Newburg, substituting shrimp for crab
meat. Since the shrimp has a more distinct flavor than crab
meat, and cannot so easily be ruined by additions, finely cut
green peppers, pimientos and mushrooms may be added if desired. The mixture may also be made less rich than for Crab
Newburg, using a thinner cream or even milk, two eggs instead
of four, and using four tablespoons of flour instead of two.

Shrimp Pilau

1 cup rice
2 cups water
½ teaspoon salt, or to taste
1 large onion, finely cut
4 tablespoons butter
1 green pepper, finely cut
1 No. 2 can tomatoes if desired
1 lb. cooked shrimp
Serves 6

Cook rice in boiling salted water until tender, about thirty minutes. Cook onion and pepper in butter until brown and tender. Add tomatoes. I myself prefer shrimp pilau without the tomatoes. Turn mixture into rice. Add shrimp. Simmer for ten minutes. This serves four to six.

Sautéd Shrimp and Okra

Use equal parts of cooked shrimp and raw, cut okra. Cut shrimp in halves. Sauté together in butter, allowing two tablespoons of butter to every cup of shrimp and okra. Salt and pepper lightly while browning. Turn two or three times. Time, about ten minutes, or until okra is brown and tender. This is good served with hominy grits.

Shrimp Salad

> 1 cup cooked shrimp, cut in pieces
> ½ cup shredded cabbage
> 1 small onion, minced
> ½ green pepper, finely cut
> ½ cup lemon-mayonnaise

Shrimp Wiggle

> 1 cup cooked shrimp, cut in pieces
> 1 small can tiny peas
> 1 cup rich cream sauce
> 1 teaspoon Worcestershire sauce

Simmer mixture until bubbling. Serve on toast.

Stone Crabs

Stone crabs are found, usually in rocky places, along the Florida coast. They are scarce, and he who has ever eaten them has feasted on a dish almost as rare as nightingales' tongues. Only the large, bulbous claws are used. I believe there is a method of baking them on top of a hot iron range, but the method with which I am familiar is by boiling twenty-five minutes in salted water. The armor-like shell is cracked off and the thick, white, sweet meat comes out almost whole. It may be eaten hot, served with melted butter and lemon. It is best served cold, with tart mayonnaise, and Cuban bread and cold ale on the side.

Florida Lobster or Crawfish

Our crawfish come usually from quite far south in the state, so that they are often known as Key West crawfish. I admit sadly that they cannot compare with the Northern lobster. The exquisite flavor is lacking and the meat is tougher and more fibrous. Yet with Maine lobster impracticable if not impossible we are grateful for our tropical substitute. I had crawfish at Bimini, in the Bahamas, small, fresh-caught, boiled, split, served with tart mayonnaise, that seemed at the moment delicious as one could ask. Crawfish are well suited to making a very good Lobster Thermidor.

Lobster Thermidor

Boil whole lobsters or crawfish about thirty minutes. Cool and split lengthwise in halves. Remove contents of shell. Cut lobster meat, including claw meat, in cubes. For the meat of two or three lobsters, make one cup of cream sauce with two tablespoons butter, two tablespoons flour and one cup thin cream, one-half teaspoon salt. To sauce, add lobster meat, one small can mushrooms, one tablespoon chopped parsley and one-third cup sherry. Fill shells with mixture. Mix together one-half cup bread crumbs and one-half cup grated cheese. Sprinkle thickly over filled shells. Dust with paprika. Bake about twenty minutes in a hot oven and brown under broiler. Serve two halves per person.

Lobster Newburg

Follow recipe for Crab Newburg.

Cold Crawfish, Lettuce Tartare
(Chef Huston)

Split cold boiled crawfish. Remove inedible portions. Fill cavity with crisp green lettuce minced fine, mixed with enough tartar sauce to make a moist mixture. This is very delicate. Homemade tartar sauce is best. Combine tart mayonnaise with finely cut dill pickle and onion.

Florida Oysters

We have satisfactory oysters in Florida, especially from Appalachicola, but, like the lobsters, they are only poor and honest relations of the Baltimore oysters. We enjoy them immensely on an outdoor oyster roast, but the delightful surroundings and congenial company are a large part of the flavor. South of St. Augustine on the Matanzas River, an old Negro fisherman lives in a shack that would delight the soul of an artist. He "raises" his own oysters, feeding the beds and gathering only the mature oysters. We like to go to Gene's on a moonlight night for an oyster roast—all one can eat for fifty cents. Gene swears he makes a profit, but I do not see how. We take our own butter for melting, condiments, bread or crackers, salad and beer or coffee.

We turn down a narrow sand road between scrub palmettos, and around a bend in the river the orange glow from Gene's fire lights the live oaks and the long pine tables. Sheet iron the size of a double bed lies over blazing fatwood. Gene brings baskets of oysters from the river bed, dumps them out on the hot sheet iron, rakes them flat, and throws over them crocus sacks wrung out of cold water. Steam rises, the oysters sizzle, and at the right mysterious moment known only to himself, Gene removes the sacks, rakes the oysters to one side with a flourish, and piles them along the tables.

"Don't hold back," Gene says. "There's more where them came from!"

Each of us is provided with an oyster knife for one hand and a large white glove for the other. The oysters open easily and we shuck them into our individual ramekins of melted butter and condiments. They are small, but with a fine tangy flavor. We eat incredible dozens.

Back of Ed Hopkins' fish chowder lies my initiation into all the delights of Florida. It was Ed, now gathered to his fathers —and may God rest his soul and provide him with some of the joys, and foods, that on earth meant Heaven to him—who introduced me to the Big Scrub and to the "South Moon Under" and "Yearling" people and country. Ed was of the great amateur cooks of this world, and with the simplest Florida backwoods ingredients and a Dutch oven, turned out dishes so superlative that when I now prepare one, I grieve that Ed is not here to partake.

In *Cross Creek* I described his fish chowder, "uncorrupted by alien elements such as peas and tomatoes, that makes a poor thing of any New England chowder." I thought that I had started another War between the States, for half of New England, it seemed to me, descended on me with disturbed and sometimes virulent letters, crying that no true New England chowder used peas and tomatoes. Somewhere in my past I had eaten Manhattan chowder, and had been misinformed as to its background. Let me here make amends, and proclaim that Ed's fish chowder is almost identical with the best New England chowder—EXCEPT that New Englanders who tried his recipe, from *Cross Creek,* wrote me humbly that his was as good or better. One generous soul wrote me that her elderly mother, a New Englander from days of the *Mayflower,* sighed on partaking of Ed's recipe and said, "Daughter, this is it. Don't ever bother again with Grandfather's receipt." Another New Englander, marooned in California, tried it and wrote that passing cars slowed down by their gate as the aroma was wafted on the air, and a multi-motored bomber overhead "dipped its wings in salute."

Ed Hopkins' Fish Chowder

1 6 to 8 lb. big-mouthed bass, or any large, firm-fleshed fish
   or
6 1½-lb. bass or perch, or any small, firm fish
½ lb. white bacon (fat salt pork)
   or, if necessary,
½ lb. breakfast bacon
2 to 3 lbs. Irish potatoes
1 lb. onions
Cream
Butter
Uneeda biscuits (hard tack is good, too)
Salt, pepper

Cut bacon in pieces about one-half inch by one-quarter inch. Place a layer in bottom of Dutch oven, by preference, or in a deep iron skillet. Fillet fish. Leave small fish in halves, or cut large boned fish into pieces about four inches by two inches. Place a layer of filleted fish above bacon. Add a layer of thinly sliced raw onion and a layer of sliced raw potatoes. Add a layer of crackers and dots of butter, salt and pepper. Repeat layers in this order until ingredients are used. Add enough hot water not quite to cover. More may be necessary as cooking proceeds. Cover tightly. After about ten minutes slip a spatula or pancake turner under bottom layer to prevent sticking and burning, and repeat once or twice again. All water must cook away from the chowder so that the bottom layer is browned. When fish and onion and potato are thoroughly tender but the fish is not disintegrated, and water has cooked away, almost cover with heated thin cream. Time, about forty-five minutes. Serves six. Channel, or blue catfish, makes a fine chowder.

When possible, if Emily Post is not in the offing, serve publicly onto individual hot plates or deep soup dishes, so that the chowder is not mixed up. Cornbread, spoonbread or cornmeal muffins are recommended with fish chowder. Zelma's Dutch oven rolls are not strictly *comme il faut,* by Southern standards, but are mighty good with it just the same.

Baked Fish with Spanish Sauce

Dress whole a large red snapper, sea-trout, bass, red fish, or any large, firm-fleshed fish available. It may be filled if desired with bread stuffing, seasoned with sage and onion. Place in well-greased baking pan. Place over and around fish Spanish sauce, reserving mushrooms and peas, basting fish every ten minutes with sauce from pan. Bake in moderate oven about one hour or until fish is tender. When done, push sauce from top of fish and spread with two tablespoons softened butter blended with one tablespoon flour. Increase heat and brown top. Remove to platter and garnish with parsley and lemon slices. Add mushrooms and peas to sauce, let cook until hot, and serve sauce separately in a bowl. Have the maid pass the fish whole, or serve at table. Allow one-half to three-quarter pound dressed fish per person.

Spanish Sauce

> 1 can tomatoes
> 1 large onion sliced thin
> 2 tablespoons Worcestershire sauce
> 1 tablespoon sugar
> 1 can tomato soup
> 1 green pepper cut fine
> 2 tablespoons lemon juice
> 1 teaspoon salt
> 1 small can tiny peas
> 1 can mushrooms

Florida Fried Fish

Pan-broiled fish are good, but in backwoods Florida we have lusty tastes. Small fish, we dress whole. Large fish, we bone and fillet. In any case, we like to dip them in salted cornmeal and drop them in deep, very hot fat. The cornmeal makes a crisper crust than the more delicate flour, and we happen to like it. With fried fish we like to serve hush-puppies, fried in the fish fat itself. The combination may not appeal to the too delicate of stomach, but I pray that this compendium of dishes shall not fall into the hands of any such, lest they perish either of disgust or frustration.

Broiled Fish

Pompano, flounder, Spanish mackerel, mullet and sea-trout are delicious broiled under or over an open flame. I dress them with lemon butter before broiling, and baste twice with the same mixture.

Boiled Mullet

Wrap whole mullet in a thin cloth. Lower into boiling salted water and simmer for twenty minutes. Turn out on hot platter and cover with sauce made of two tablespoons butter, two tablespoons flour, one and one-half cups hot water, the juice of one lemon, salt and pepper to taste.

Orange Lake Frog-Legs

Wash frog-legs thoroughly. They should preferably be of the previous night's catch. Place in deep pan, sprinkle with two tablespoons lemon juice or vinegar to every pound of frog-legs, and cover with small pieces of ice. Let stand in ice box from one to three hours. Rinse. Roll in lightly salted flour. Dip in beaten whole egg, then roll in fine bread crumbs. Sauté, turning once, in one-half inch of Dora's butter, until a chestnut brown. Serve at once, garnished with water cress or parsley. Tartar sauce if desired. Allow six small pairs of legs or three jumbo pairs per person. Chef Houston dips frog-legs in an egg batter and fries in deep fat, but the Cross Creek way is better.

My artist friend Robert claims to have from his student days in Paris a superb French recipe for frog-legs in garlic sauce. He becomes evasive whenever I suggest that he do the dish. Even if he does have such a recipe, frog-legs seem to me of too delicate a flavor for the use of garlic. Garlic, like perfume, must be used with discretion and on the proper occasions.

Game and Meats

The other day I sat in a hotel with friends, planning a wild Mallard duck dinner menu for their consumption later at Cross Creek. A lieutenant sat nearby. He was introduced, and he confessed that he had overheard our plans.

"I never," he said, "listened to a more *voluptuous* conversation."

My wild duck dinner sounds good, it is good, and I think ruefully that it should be good. It not only costs me as much to feed my flock of wild Mallards as to feed two mules, but it makes me ill to kill them for the table. I should never do it, except that the flock so multiplies each year that I cannot afford to keep them all. Fortunately, there are always far too many drakes, so several times a year, having given away as many as possible to new homes, I serve the excess—reluctantly—to a favored few.

Six years ago I had a gift of a setting of wild Mallard eggs from the Carolina marshes. I hatched them under a hen. The original ten ducklings lived a year in the pen. I could not endure their captivity any longer and turned them loose, expecting them to fly at once to the adjacent marshes of Orange Lake. They refused to leave. They are the lords of my manor, gay, noisy and demanding. The ten grew at one time to seventy, which is a lot of ducks. I try to keep the flock down to twenty-five.

My Mallard dinner is especially good, I think, because of the dishes served with the meat, and because the ducks, from their type of feeding, have a finer flavor than either domestic ducks or truly wild ducks. They have an abundance of skimmed milk and clabber along with their grain and their greens. This tenderizes and lightens the meat. They are fatter than the hunter's wild ducks, but not so fat as market ducks.

I am at violent variance with the school of believers in raw or under-done duck. These insist that well-done duck is bound to be hard and dry. Mine are not. The skin is crisp and crusty, the meat is moist and so tender and yielding that it may be cut with a fork. It melts on the tongue like broiled chicken liver. The ducks must be properly aged—after dressing—from three to five days, without freezing. The flavor needs no embellishment, and I do not even use the conventional onion or celery or apple stuffing. I place them, dressed whole, salted and peppered, breast side up, in a tightly covered roasting pan with an

inch of hot water in the pan. The oven is hot, four hundred and
fifty degrees, for the first fifteen minutes. The heat is then re
duced to three hundred and fifty degrees for the remaining
time of cooking. Young ducks will roast in a little over an hour
For old ducks, I allow from two to three hours. They should be
basted every fifteen minutes with the liquid in the pan. I allow
one-half duck per person. An occasional guest can eat a whole
duck, but is not encouraged.

A light, rather acid first course is desirable, such as iced
melon with lime juice or baked sherried grapefruit. With the
ducks I serve giblet gravy, wild rice, braised whole white
onions, tiny cornmeal muffins, carrot soufflé or sweet potato
in orange baskets or orange fritters, crisp celery, a tart jelly
such as currant, wild grape or wild plum or kumquat, a light
green salad, such as endive and water cress, with a trace of
minced shallots and a tart French dressing made with Tarra
gon vinegar, any good dry red wine, preferably Burgundy, and
again a light, rather acid dessert, such as tangerine sherbet.

I disremember, as we say at the Creek, just when I began
shooting chickens for the table. They were my own chickens
They were, and are, game chickens. The breed suits me to a T
because I like to see them running loose instead of cooped in a
pen. They are decorative, they take care of themselves except
for scratch feed night and morning, they roost in the orange
trees, from which the handsome bronze and red rooster assists
the coming of the dawn, and they make frying-size chickens
with large meaty breasts, earlier than any other breed. But they
are wild as hawks. When there is a man working on the place
or small pickaninnies visiting, it is rather a lark to run one
down for the pot. Spectators cheer.

But a hot summer day found old Martha and me alone, with

company coming, and we ran chickens until we dropped from exhaustion, and never touched a feather. I remembered that in Alaska my brother and I shot ruffed grouse with rifles, for the birds would not stir from their perches in distant trees across thick ravines, and, once moved to action, were gone instantly behind impenetrable Alaskan foliage so that a wing shot was out of the question. We needed the meat, and it was entirely sporting and made a difficult long shot to use a rifle and aim for the head or neck. When I got back my breath, I loaded my .22 rifle and potted the necessary broilers through the heads.

Came a day when, from too frequent shooting, I had only to appear in the yard with my .22, to have every chicken on the place scatter for the distant woods. I stalked like a panther. When I came within range, the young rooster I was after moved his head every time I fired. A dignified professor and his haughty wife were coming for dinner. I was desperate. I returned to the house for my shotgun and ignominiously, violating all rules of sportsmanship, brought down my bird. Dinner went off nicely, and the professor's grave face brightened as he bit into the succulent breast of chicken, pan-browned and oven-baked in sherry. There was a grinding noise, the professor blanched, and he removed his mouthful of chicken breast and poked at it with his fork. Two little lead pellets rolled to the plate. If it had been one little lead pellet, I should have insinuated that he had best consult his dentist. There were two. It was one of the cowardly moments in my life. I rang for more wine and asked the professor's opinion on James Joyce. There are, simply, people to whom one can explain that one shoots chickens for the table and people to whom one cannot——

Squab-Size Roast Chicken

I have a favorite way of preparing squab-sized chickens, one to one and one-quarter pounds in weight.

For every small whole chicken, prepare stuffing made of one-third cup of dry bread crumbs, sautéd in one tablespoon of butter, and two tablespoons coarsely broken pecan meats. Stuff chickens (or squabs), roll in salted and peppered flour, brown to a golden color in Dora's butter. Place in a casserole or roaster. Drain off from frying pan all but four to six tablespoons of the cooking butter, according to number of chickens. Add two cups boiling water to remaining fat, stirring well to gather up all the browned particles. Pour over chickens. Add one-quarter cup dry sherry for every chicken. Cover tightly and cook in oven at three hundred and fifty degrees until thoroughly tender, about one to one and one-half hours. It is sometimes necessary to add more hot water, as there should be a thin gravy. Fluffy rice is especially good with this dish.

I prepare quail, doves, rabbit, squirrel and even the coarser cuts of venison in this fashion, especially if the age of the game is uncertain. For doves and quail, one-quarter cup of buttered bread crumbs and one tablespoon of pecan meats for stuffing is sufficient. For rabbit, squirrel and venison I use no stuffing, but increase the quantity of hot water, the resulting gravy to be thickened with a little flour and a little chopped parsley added.

I once even prepared, lacking game, a piece of beef in this manner. The occasion irks me still. My friend Phil May asked to bring his friend, Wallace Stevens, the poet, to dinner at Cross Creek. The great man was on a strict diet, he wrote, and must be served only lean meat, a green salad and fruit. I planned my best baked-in-sherry-ham for the rest of the company, and wracked my brains for a method of making of lean meat a delicacy. I decided to prepare the heart of a Boston pot roast of beef in an individual casserole, with sherry. The poet proved delightful but condescending. He began on his beef, looked over at the clove-stuck ham, and announced that he would partake not only of that, but of all the other rich dishes on the table. His diet, it seemed, was not for purposes of health, but for vanity. He was, simply, reducing. I snatched his sherried beef from him, pulled out the bone and tossed it on the hearth to my pointer dog.

Smother-Fried Quail, Dove, Rabbit, Squirrel

I use this method when the game is of uncertain age. Roll the game in salted and peppered flour. Drop in a Dutch oven or deep iron skillet containing one-quarter inch of butter. Brown on all sides. Almost cover with boiling water. Cover tightly and let simmer over open flame or campfire until meat is meltingly tender. Thicken gravy with flour. More salt will be needed.

Deep-Fried Young Quail or Young Dove

Dip quail or dove in milk. Roll well in salted and peppered flour. Drop in kettle of fat hot enough to brown a cube of bread in sixty seconds. Fry until a chestnut brown. Serve with hot grits and butter.

Pan-Fried Young Quail or Dove

Roll quail or dove in salted and peppered flour. Fry in one-half inch of hot butter until tender, turning once. Make gravy by adding flour to butter, one tablespoon flour to every two tablespoons of butter, and rich milk or thin cream, one cup to every tablespoon of flour. More salt.

My friend Dessie is one of Florida's most expert campers. Given an axe and a gun, she can make a good living in the woods. I once saw her bring down a duck on the wing with a .22 rifle. As a cook, I should be extremely cautious about turning her loose in my kitchen, but on a camp, I should take her say-so as to the cooking of any game dish.

How to Fry Venison
(Dessie)

Cut chops, or backstrap, three-quarters of an inch thick, rub with lemon and sprinkle with flour. In an uncovered Dutch oven or iron skillet melt one tablespoon butter and one tablespoon Crisco. Have pan only medium hot over low coals. Add venison and fry six to ten minutes, turning only once. Salt and pepper when done.

Venison is also delicious broiled like steak. It should be aged.

Dessie also gave me gravely a recipe that she calls "Coot Surprise." My comment was that I should be surprised as all getout if anybody could eat it. I myself consider coots completely inedible. Even Webster's dictionary backs me up in low-rating coots, and says, "They are stupid, and fly slowly, and can hardly be classed as game birds." I have prepared coots hopefully according to all sorts of varying backwoods advice, and always had to throw them out, with the exception of pilau of rice and coot livers and gizzards. But there are many, including Dessie, who consider them good. For the curious, experimentally inclined, here is her recipe.

Coot Surprise

Skin coots and rub with salt and lemon juice or vinegar. Let stand overnight. Wash, split in halves, and rub with salt and pepper. Dust with flour. Fry in medium deep hot fat in a covered pan until golden brown. Serve with wild rice and green vegetables or a green salad.

Jugged Rabbit

Cut rabbit in pieces. Place in deep pan and cover with red wine, to which is added one teaspoon whole cloves, one teaspoon allspice, two bay leaves, one teaspoon whole peppercorns. Let stand in cool place for three days. Drain. Roll in salted and peppered flour. Brown in one-quarter inch butter. Cover with hot water and simmer until tender. More hot water may be necessary. Remove rabbit. Stir in one tablespoon flour dissolved in four tablespoons cold water for every cup of gravy. Add one-half teaspoon salt, dash of pepper. Pour over rabbit. One rabbit serves four to six.

Bear Meat

Bears, once so plentiful in Florida that before 1792 William Bartram wrote, "there are still far too many bears in Florida," are becoming scarce. I see no reason for destroying the remaining ones, since they live so far from any domestic clearing that they are no longer a menace, as formerly, to stock. But I must admit that bear meat at the proper season, and properly cooked, is a delicious meat. A male bear in the mating season, like a boar hog, is not fit to eat. A female nursing bear not only has tough and stringy meat, but for humanitarian reasons should never be destroyed. A young male bear in the off-season provides meat better than the best beef. I should happily settle for a stupid steer, but on the occasions when I have had bear meat in the Big Scrub of Florida, I have enjoyed it thoroughly.

Pot Roast of Bear

Place haunch or chuck of bear meat, salted and peppered, in a covered roasting pan with one inch of hot water and one-quarter cup of melted bear fat. Roast in a hot oven, four hundred to four hundred and fifty degrees, basting every fifteen minutes, until tender, from two to four hours. Remove meat from roaster. Stir in flour and extra salt and pepper to browned fat in pan, and add hot water to make gravy of proper consistency. Serve with hominy grits, boiled onions and swamp cabbage.

Bear Steak

Hang rib steaks of bear as long as possible without spoiling. Brush with salt and pepper and melted bear fat or olive oil. Broil over hot live oak coals about twenty minutes, turning twice. Serve with baked sweet potatoes and cole slaw.

Alligator - Tail Steak

Rattlesnake meat is canned commercially in Florida and served as a delicate hors-d'œuvre. I have never tried it and do not intend to. It is said to taste much like canned tuna. *Chacun à son goût.* Bartram wrote in his famous *Travels* that Governor Grant of Florida had a passion for rattlesnake meat "if the snake had not bit himself," but Bartram, as I should have done, "tasted of the meat but could not swallow it."

Steak from the tail of an alligator is another matter. It is truly delicious. It is like liver or veal (which it resembles in texture and coloring) in that it must be cooked very quickly or a very long time. In between, it toughens. Cut strips lengthwise of the tail, four inches long and two inches wide, or cut cross-sections between the vertebræ. Roll in salted and peppered flour and fry quickly in butter. It may also be browned in the butter, hot water and the juice of a lemon added, and simmered for two to two and one-half hours until tender.

A woman wrote me from Mississippi that she and her twelve-year-old son, a great hunter, had read my chapter on foods in *Cross Creek.* A few days later, the young man came on an eight-foot alligator in a Mississippi swamp, and horrified her by dragging it home for her to cook the tail. She wrote that at the moment she was torn between attempting it, and burying the alligator, to face her young son's wrath.

Veal Chops or Cutlet in Sherry

Dip veal chops or cutlet in salted and peppered flour, then in beaten egg, then in fine bread crumbs. Place in iron skillet in one-half inch of hot butter. Brown on both sides. Almost cover with boiling water. Add the juice of one lemon. Cover tightly. Let simmer until tender, adding more hot water if necessary. Time, about two hours. When done, add one-half cup dry sherry and simmer five minutes. Remove veal. Thicken remaining liquid with flour if necessary and extra salt to make gravy. Pour over veal on serving dish and garnish with parsley. The same method is also delicious by omitting the sherry, but adding one tablespoon Worcestershire sauce at the same time as the lemon juice. Allow one-third to one-half pound veal per person.

Lamb Kidneys with Sherry

6 lamb kidneys
1 tablespoon butter
1 tablespoon flour
½ teaspoon salt
¾ cup hot water
2 tablespoons dry sherry

Skin kidneys, remove membranes, and cut in pieces about three-quarters of an inch by one-half inch. Sauté five minutes in sizzling hot butter over a hot flame, turning twice. Stir in flour and salt and let brown one minute. Stir in hot water slowly and simmer two minutes. Add sherry and serve at once on thin toast, or with waffles or omelet. Serves two.

Flank Steak

Score a one and one-half pound flank steak in a diamond pattern. Have a deep iron skillet smoking hot. Brown steak well on both sides, using no fat. Add one and one-half cups boiling water and one-half teaspoon whole peppercorns. Cover tightly and simmer slowly one and one-half hours.

Add one cup boiling water, one teaspoon salt, and surround with whole carrots and whole onions. Cover and simmer one hour. It will be necessary to add at least one more cup of boiling water. There should be two cups of gravy. When steak and vegetables are thoroughly tender, remove to hot platter and thicken gravy with two level tablespoons flour dissolved in four tablespoons cold water.

This makes a very good and inexpensive one-dish meal for four. Small whole potatoes may be added one-half hour before end if desired. Or, serve with mashed potatoes.

Pork or Ham Baked in Milk

Place pork chops or a thick slice of center-cut ham in an iron skillet. Cover with cold sweet milk, preferably skimmed. Salt lightly (ham will probably require no salt), and pepper. Place in moderate oven and bake uncovered until meat is extremely tender, about two hours. As skin forms on milk and browns, stir in, repeating until liquid has disappeared and the fat accumulated in the pan has well browned. It may be necessary if meat is not tender by this time, to add from one-half to one cup of boiling water. Remove meat to hot serving platter. Drain off any fat in pan above two tablespoons, stir in one and one-quarter tablespoons flour and add one cup milk slowly, stirring. Simmer two minutes. Salt if needed. Pour milk gravy over meat or serve separately in gravy boat.

It is convenient and economical to plan a meal baked altogether in the oven. With this dish, I usually serve baked sweet potatoes, cornmeal muffins, and baked apples or escalloped apples or Brown Betty as the dessert.

Baked Peanut Ham with Sherry

Florida or Georgia peanut-fed ham has, to my notion, the finest flavor of any ham. I admire the well-aged Kentucky, Tennessee and Virginia country ham, but I am not an addict. This is purely a matter of personal taste. I happen to prefer a moist, juicy ham to a dry one. Moreover, the choice old country hams are so valuable and valued that one feels guilty in eating as much as one wishes, and is expected to nibble daintily on wafer-thin wisps. This convention once ended a friendship of long standing. A friend had an old Kentucky ham as the *pièce de résistance* at a Christmas buffet supper. She was horrified to discover a respectable lawyer standing at the buffet board, hacking off half-pound wedges of the sacred ham, and eating as fast as he hacked.

"I never," he said fatuously, "ate such delicious ham."

He was never invited to her house again.

Peanut-fed ham—or any good market variety—in sherry, is not as expensive as it sounds, and well worth any extra trouble and cost. A country ham must be soaked over-night in cold water. Other hams need no soaking. Place in a deep kettle with cold water to cover. Add one-half cup maple syrup or honey, or brown sugar, one teaspoon whole cloves, one-quarter teaspoon whole allspice, four bay leaves, and one cup of dry wine. I prefer, in order, sherry, Burgundy, claret. Actually, any wine is good, even a home-made wine, provided that it is not sweet. Cider is also good. There are so many good and very inexpen-

sive domestic wines on the market that the added expense is
scarcely an item. Cover the kettle tightly. Bring very slowly to
a boil, then turn fire very low and let simmer gently until ham
is very tender but not disintegrating—about twenty minutes to
the pound, or four hours for a twelve-pound ham. A large ham
takes a little longer than twenty minutes to the pound. Let cool
in the water in which it was cooked. Remove skin. Cover fatty
top one-quarter inch thick with a mixture of fine bread crumbs,
brown sugar and sherry, using about one cup of crumbs to one-
half cup of brown sugar and enough sherry just to hold mixture together, so that it may be patted in shape without running
off. Stick with whole cloves one inch apart. Brown in hot oven,
moderating oven when ham is brown and allowing one-half
hour longer if ham is to be served hot. It is probably best served
cold, as the tender meat is less likely to shred when cut. I carve
it inelegantly in quarter-inch thick slices, as I have found folk
grateful for such a quantity.

Brunswick Stew

The origin of this dish, dear to the South, is uncertain. It is
here and there believed that it came from Brunswick, Georgia,
yet lifted eyebrows greet a request for the dish in inns of that
small city. A correspondent who has lived much abroad wrote
me that the dish was a favorite of Queen Victoria, and since that
late, great queen clung faithfully to her German origins, my
correspondent believes, as do I, that its source must have been
Brunswick in old Germany. The recipe varies in every section of
the South. The Duchess of Windsor gives a very good recipe,
using chicken, tomatoes, okra, corn, string beans and potatoes.

At Cross Creek and in the neighboring Florida backwoods, we make the dish at hog-killing time, and associate it with that autumn season of harvest and plenty. The basis is fresh pork, and is likely to consist, in humbler circles, of small pieces of lean pork that have escaped the sausage grinder, along with the liver, the lights, and the heart, cut in one-half-inch cubes. Since I cook emotionally, without measurement, and since I am compiling this set of recipes in the heart of the summer, when no decent Floridian would dream of killing a hog, and so cannot "prove" my measurements as I have done with other recipes, I can give only approximate proportions. At any time after the middle of November, I should be glad to supply any one with access to fresh pork with the exact measurements, provided that he or she writes me out of a sincere need and not idle curiosity.

Roughly, the proportions are as follows:

> **4 lbs. lean fresh pork, liver, lights, heart,**
> **   all cut in ½-inch cubes**
> **Simmer until tender, 2 to 3 hours, in 4 quarts**
> **   of water**
> **Add**
> **2 teaspoons salt**
> **⅛ teaspoon black pepper**
> **1 large can peas (or 2 cups cooked cow-peas)**
> **1 small can lima beans**
> **1 large can tomatoes**
> **1 medium can corn**
> **Serves 8 to 10**

Simmer until mixture is rather thick. It should be moist, but not actually wet. Cornbread should be served as a concomitant. Plain people enjoy breaking the cornbread into the stew.

Chili Con Carne

3 lbs. lean beef cut in ½ to ¾ inch cubes
4 onions cut fine
1 tablespoon minced garlic
Brown together in ½ cup olive oil or Wesson oil
    with 2 tablespoons olive oil added for flavor
Add 4 qts. hot water
1 large can tomatoes
1 tablespoon allspice, powdered
2 tablespoons salt
3 tablespoons paprika
3 tablespoons chili powder
Simmer 4 hours
Add 2 cans red kidney beans. Simmer 20 minutes

This is as fine a chili con carne as I have ever tasted. The quantity obviously serves a party of about ten, but since it is just as good warmed over, and will keep well in the ice box, I usually make the full quantity.

Steak and Kidney Pie

Since my Michigan farm ancestors have put me in the habit of serving more food than can be eaten, I always have steak left over. I probably have steak and kidney pie in the back of my mind. Sometimes I get hungry for the dish and buy round steak especially for the purpose. Any left-over beef, from a rib roast or a pot roast, is also good. The proportion of steak to kidneys is flexible. The recipe is anything but rigid, and if I have a cup of steak-meat, I buy only three or four lamb kidneys or one veal kidney. If I have a half-cup of steak, I buy six or eight lamb kidneys, two veal kidneys, or a beef kidney. In any case, two cups of diced meat are sufficient to serve four to six when baked in the finished pie.

Brown the diced cooked steak or beef and diced kidneys in two tablespoons of butter to every cup of meat. I use a deep, narrow kettle. Add one cup boiling water for every cup of meat. Cover tightly and let simmer about two hours, or until meat is almost tender. Add one-half teaspoon salt to every cup of meat, a dash of pepper, one cup boiling water, two carrots cut in strips lengthwise and four small whole onions. Cover and simmer fifteen minutes. Add one medium-sized peeled raw potato quartered, to every cup of meat. Cover and simmer fifteen minutes more. More hot water may be needed. Thicken gravy with one tablespoon flour in two tablespoons cold water for every cup of meat. Have ready a rich biscuit mixture—the following to cover a casserole or baking dish six inches in diameter:

> 2 cups flour
> 5 teaspoons baking powder
> 4 tablespoons butter (or part Crisco)
> 1 teaspoon salt
> 1 cup milk (or enough to roll out dough)

Sift dry ingredients together. Work in shortening with fingers until mixture is like coarse meal. Cut in milk with knife. Turn on well-floured board, fold over twice, and roll to one-half inch in thickness, or until mixture will cover top of baking dish with an overhang of one-half inch. Turn meat and vegetable mixture into casserole or baking dish, cover with biscuit crust, cut several lines in crust as for top-crust of any pie, and bake twenty minutes in a hot oven, or until crust is well browned.

Almost any left-over meat may be used in this fashion, with the vegetables, to make a delicious pie that is a one-dish meal.

Blackbird Pie

This dish is illegal, since the taking of red-winged blackbirds is forbidden by Federal law—which I discovered probably just in time to save myself a term in the penitentiary. But I made it often in lean days at the Creek, and since it is so delicious, and since any small birds may be substituted for the red-winged blackbirds, such as ricebirds (legal in season), quail, dove, or one-pound-size chickens, I list it.

Brown the whole dressed birds in one tablespoon butter to every bird. Cover with hot water. Add one bay leaf, one teaspoon salt and a dash of pepper. Simmer until tender, tightly covered. Add one carrot cut in strips and two small whole onions to every bird. Simmer fifteen minutes. Add one small raw potato, diced, to every bird. Simmer fifteen minutes more. More hot water may be needed, as gravy should cover mixture. Thicken gravy with one tablespoon flour dissolved in two tablespoons cold water to every cup of gravy. Place mixture in casserole, add two tablespoons chopped parsley, one-quarter cup sherry to every bird, and cover with biscuit crust as for steak and kidney pie. Bake in hot oven twenty minutes or until well browned. Four birds per person are right, so that for six people, one has truly "four and twenty blackbirds baked in a pie."

Spanish Chicken Fricassee

From Mrs. Hansen in California, I have this very hot, very delicious recipe. For a highly seasoned recipe, I have found it superb. This serves six to eight.

1 4 to 5-lb. fricassee chicken

Cut in pieces, cover with cold water, add one teaspoon salt, and simmer until the meat falls from the bones—two to three hours. Let cool. Remove meat from bones. Skim fat from stock. Strain stock.

Boil four red peppers in water to cover until tender. Remove seeds. Chop peppers. Save the water in which they were boiled.

Boil one quart tomatoes, canned or fresh, two minced cloves

of garlic and four finely cut onions together until tender. Put through a colander.

Add chicken stock, chopped peppers and pepper water to the tomato mixture. To every tablespoon of the skimmed chicken fat, add one and one-half tablespoons flour and brown together. Stir into sauce. Add salt, chili powder and any ground hot pepper powder, to taste.

Put chicken in casserole. Cover with sauce. Sprinkle with grated Parmesan cheese. Heat thoroughly in oven.

Mrs. Hansen writes that half beef and half pork, done in the same fashion and with the same sauce, makes Enchiladas. I have not tried it, but if it is as good as the Spanish fricassee chicken, it is bound to be all right.

Mrs. Hansen's Tortillas

1 cup flour
½ cup cornmeal
¼ teaspoon salt
1 egg
Enough water to make a thin paste
Serves 4 to 6

Spread very thin in two- or three-inch cakes on hot, ungreased griddle. Bake on both sides. Place tortillas on platter, spread with ground cooked beef, chicken or pork, roll up, and pour over a sauce made of strained tomatoes cooked with garlic or onion and hot pepper until thick. Garnish with grated cheese and chopped young green onions.

Yellow Rice and Chicken
(Arroz Con Pollo)

1 frying size chicken
1 onion
Pinch of saffron
1 cup olive oil
2 pimientos
2 teaspoons salt
1½ quarts water
2 buttons garlic
1 bay leaf
1 lb. rice (cooked)
1 2-oz. can Petit Pois
1 green pepper
6 oz. tomatoes, canned or fresh
Serves 4 generously

Cut chicken in quarters and fry in olive oil (Wesson oil if necessary) with sliced onion and garlic. When brown and tender, add tomatoes and water. Simmer for five minutes. Add bay leaf, salt, cooked rice, saffron and chopped green pepper. Stir thoroughly. Place in moderate oven for twenty minutes. Garnish with tiny peas and strips of pimientos. This is a famous recipe from the Cuban restaurant, the Columbia, in Tampa.

Southern Hash

My friend Norton once remarked that he was extremely fond of hash. I invited him to the Creek to partake with me. I served with pride a beautifully browned omelet-like dry hash, which was what I had been brought up on. He ate it sadly. Time proved that what he called "hash" is what I should call a finely cut, wet stew. To distinguish, I now call it Southern hash. It is very good, very economical, and I make it frequently. These proportions serve three to four.

> 1 cup left-over beef, cut in small cubes
> 1 cup raw potatoes, cut in small cubes
> 1 or 2 onions, cut fine
> 1 green pepper, cut fine

Brown beef and onions together in two tablespoons butter. Add two cups boiling water and the potatoes and green pepper. Salt and pepper to taste. Cover and let cook slowly until all ingredients are tender. The hash should have plenty of gravy, and more hot water may be needed. A small amount of flour thickening may be added when done. Serve on toast, or preferably with soft grits.

Dumplings

> 1½ cups flour
> 2 teaspoons baking powder
> ¾ teaspoon salt
> 1 egg
> ½ cup milk

Sift dry ingredients together. Combine well-beaten egg and milk. Stir into dry ingredients. Beat well. Drop by large tablespoonfuls on gently boiling chicken. Cover. Steam without disturbing for twelve minutes. Thicken chicken gravy with a little flour dissolved in a little cold water. Serve with mashed potatoes. Serves six.

Chicken and Dumplings

1 4 to 5-lb. fricassee chicken
Serves 5 to 6

Cut in pieces, cover with hot water. Add two stalks of celery and one teaspoon salt. Simmer until very tender, about two or three hours. Remove celery. Drop in dumplings.

Spaghetti and Meat Balls

I had assumed that every cook had a good spaghetti recipe. I include mine only on the insistence of Idella that it is unusually good. This serves four to six.

1 lb. round steak ground twice
or
¾ lb. veal and ¼ lb. lean pork, ground twice together
2 medium to large onions, diced
2 cloves garlic, minced

2 tablespoons parsley

¼ cup olive oil (Wesson oil will do)

1 can tomatoes, sieved

1 small can tomato paste

1 teaspoon salt

Pepper to taste

Heat olive oil in deep iron skillet. Cook onions and garlic in the fat until a golden brown. Add the sieved tomatoes and tomato paste, salt and pepper. Cover and let simmer gently at least an hour.

Shape ground meat into small round balls, to which has been added the chopped parsley and one-quarter teaspoon salt and a little pepper. Brown well on all sides in a smoking hot iron skillet, without fat. Turn into this skillet the cooked sauce. Another small can of sieved tomatoes may be added at this stage if sauce seems too thick. Simmer for two or three minutes.

Half an hour before sauce and meat balls are ready, prepare a deep kettle of rapidly boiling salted water. Drop in slowly one-half pound spaghetti. Partially cover, with lid to one side. Boil rapidly for twenty minutes. Drain spaghetti in colander. Turn out on hot platter and pour over the sauce and meat balls. Sprinkle generously with grated Parmesan cheese and serve extra grated cheese. The secret of good Italian spaghetti is plenty of sauce and plenty of cheese.

This also makes a good one-dish meal. Red wine and a green salad with tart French dressing make the perfect accompaniment.

Guinea Hen in Dutch Oven

Dress guinea hen whole. Bread stuffing with onion and sage may be used if desired. Cover breast and legs with a paste made of one-quarter cup flour, one-quarter cup butter and one-half teaspoon salt. Place breast side up in a Dutch oven, or on side. Add two cups hot water. Cover with Dutch oven lid, on which is scattered a thin layer of hot live-oak coals. Place Dutch oven over low coals. Keep fire low but steady on both top and bottom. It may be necessary to add more hot water to prevent burning. When breast browns, use no more coals on lid. After half an hour of baking, place small whole carrots and medium-sized whole peeled potatoes around guinea hen. Continue baking an hour more. If guinea hen seems to have any tendency to toughness, hold up on the addition of vegetables until it shows signs of becoming tender. All water should cook off, so that fat in bottom of oven browns. Stir two tablespoons flour and one-half teaspoon salt into two cups water until smooth. Pour slowly around guinea hen, stirring until gravy thickens. Cook one minute. Serve guinea hen and vegetables directly from Dutch oven.

Turtles and Gophers

Ed and Jean Hopkins introduced me to turtle and cooter and I have blessed them ever since. We have five varieties of turtle in Florida—the rather scarce sea turtle, the hard-shell inland turtle, the alligator cooter, or turtle, the soft-shell cooter, and the so-called "gopher," actually a dusty land turtle. The alligator turtle is close kin to the hard-shell turtle, and perhaps the whitest and sweetest of any of the turtle meats. The alligator turtle takes its name from the ridged shell. It is a vicious creature with an evil beak that can make mince-meat of the hands of the unwary.

Preparing any of the hard-shelled turtles for cooking is the most difficult part of the process. The hard shell must be cut away from the meat, a job calling sometimes for an axe and always for a strong hand. The entrails are discarded, the liver and eggs, if any, being retained. The clawed feet are scalded in boiling water until the tough skin and claws can be slipped off from the meat. The meat is then cut in pieces two to four inches in size and parboiled until thoroughly tender. Add three-quarters teaspoon salt when partly done. Drain. Dip each piece separately in egg batter.

Egg Batter

½ cup flour
⅛ teaspoon salt
5 tablespoons milk
2 egg yolks, beaten
2 teaspoons olive oil (or Wesson oil)
2 egg whites beaten stiff

Drop batter-covered turtle in deep very hot fat, or in very hot fat to cover in a deep iron skillet.

Soft-shell cooter is prepared in the same way, except that the gelatinous outer edge of the soft shell is scalded until the thin skin can be rubbed off, then cut in two- to four-inch pieces and parboiled with the meat. It is dipped also in the egg batter and deep fried. It has an utterly delicious texture and flavor, but is somehow so rich that no more than two portions should be eaten, under penalty of indigestion. I prefer turtle to fried chicken.

The turtle eggs of all varieties, including the sea turtle, are a great delicacy. Here and there a Floridian turns up his nose at them, foolishly. Old colored Martha shares my passion for turtle and turtle eggs. I often stop by the road to capture a passing turtle for her, my price for my trouble being always a share of the eggs. They are about the size of golf balls. They are boiled in heavily salted water twenty minutes. The white never solidifies, but the hard-boiled yolk is rich, rather grainy, with a fine and distinct flavor. They are eaten "out of hand," from the shell, breaking off the top of the shell, dotting the egg with salt and pepper and butter, and popping the contents of the shell directly into the mouth. A dozen turtle eggs, with plain bread and butter and a glass of ale, make all I ask of a light luncheon or supper.

The deep-sea turtles lay in summer at the foot of the sand dunes along our coast, so cleverly that only the expert can find the eggs. I have watched a three-hundred-pound turtle lumber in from the sea on a moonlit July night, crawl slowly to the foot of a dune, leaving a track that looks as though a small tractor had passed, dig her nest with her flippers, lay her eggs over a period of a couple of hours, cover the nest and pack down the sand with her hind flippers—and still been hard put to it to find the eggs. Perhaps two feet under the main cavity dug for the nest, she has hollowed a narrow passage at a sharp angle, and here lie the eggs. I have counted as many as one hundred and thirty-five. Conservationists make a habit of leaving at least half of the eggs in the nest. The selfish and greedy take them all, and the criminal have been known to kill the turtle and take out the eggs, rather than discommode themselves by waiting for her to lay. There is now a hundred-dollar fine for this ruthless practice, but the perpetrators are hard to catch.

A turtle-digger ran afoul of martial law the other night, near my ocean cottage. A jeep patrols our beach at night, the beach being closed to all traffic. The turtle-hunter had found the tell-tale tractorlike trail, the rounded nest, and was digging as busily as a badger. Footsteps crunched on the sand behind him, and a soldier from the jeep stood over him with a flourished gun.

"Who the h— are you? What are you doing?"

"Why, I'm digging turtle eggs."

The soldier was from the inland North. The digger must certainly be a saboteur burying dynamite. Patiently, the digger explained the habits of the sea turtles.

"Well, brother," said the Yank, "you damn well better *find* turtle eggs."

In St. Augustine there is a large Minorcan population. In the early days of Florida a Doctor Turnbull imported a colony from the island of Minorca near Spain, to work with him on his plantations near what is now New Smyrna. He counted on indigo to make his fortune and treated the Minorcans as slaves. His project failed and the doctor abandoned them to their own resources. They fell at last, half-starved, into good hands, had their contract with the doctor voided, and were assigned land in and around St. Augustine. Their descendants are there today, reputable property owners, and with a choice assortment of old Spanish and Minorcan dishes in their repertoire. I wish that I had more recipes of these foods to offer. The only one I have been given, have tried and for which I can give the recipe, is gopher stew. It is superb.

Minorcan Gopher Stew

Wash the decapitated gopher. Cut the shell away from the meat. Scald the feet until the skin and claws can be removed. Discard entrails. Cut meat in two-inch pieces. Simmer until thoroughly tender in two cups water to every cup of meat, adding one-half teaspoon salt and a dash of pepper to every cup of meat.

In a deep kettle or Dutch oven, heat fat, preferably olive oil, allowing one-quarter cup of fat to every cup of meat. Brown in fat one large chopped onion to every cup of meat, one small can of tomatoes and one green pepper, finely cut. Simmer gently while gopher is cooking. More tomatoes may be added if mixture cooks down too much. When gopher is tender, turn the sauce into the gopher pot. There should be enough liquid to make plenty of gravy. Thicken by mashing the yolks of hard-boiled eggs, two eggs to every cup of meat, and stirring into the stew. Add more salt and pepper to taste. Stir in three tablespoons dry sherry to every cup of meat. Serve at once, preferably directly from pot.

Thin corn sticks make a good bread to serve with the stew, and spring onions, ripe olives and a green salad usually accompany it.

Pilaus

The pilau has travelled a long way to backwoods Florida from its sources in Turkey and adjacent countries, where it is the pilaf. It seems likely that the Moors took it to Spain and the Spaniards to Florida. William Bartram found it here on his travels and spelled it "pillo." We pronounce the word "pur-loo." It is any dish of meat and rice cooked together. No Florida church supper, no large rural gathering, is without it. It is blessed among dishes for such a purpose, or for a large family, for meat goes farther in a pilau than prepared in any other way. I once visited a girls' camp in the Adirondacks when the tragedy occurred of only one chicken being delivered, instead of three. I suggested a pilau. Like the loaves and fishes, it fed the multitude. No one got more than a small bit of chicken, but the good flavor was all through the rich rice. One cup of finished pilau is a serving.

Chicken or Fresh Pork Pilau

Cut large fricassee chicken in pieces as for frying. Loin or shoulder of pork is cut in chops. Cover well with water and cook slowly until meat is tender. Add salt and pepper to taste. Most Southerners like a pilau highly peppered. Add washed uncooked rice. There should be three cups of liquid to every cup of uncooked rice. Cover, stir once, and cook over a low fire until rice is tender and has absorbed the liquid, about twenty or twenty-five minutes. Hard-boiled eggs are sometimes cut into pilau when done.

Ox-Tail Pilau

Boil one or two ox-tails with two sliced onions and one cut green pepper in salted water until meat is tender. Add uncooked rice, allowing the same proportion of three cups of stock to one cup of rice. When rice is tender and has absorbed the stock, stir in one can of tomatoes, more salt if necessary, black pepper, heat thoroughly, and serve.

Coot Liver and Gizzard Pilau

A coot liver and gizzard pilau is made simply by cooking available coot livers and gizzards with enough rice to feed as many people as need feeding!

Shrimp Pilau

Shrimp pilau needs the addition of some fat. This is best found, to Florida tastes, in dicing fine one slice of white bacon (salt pork) to each cup of shrimps and frying it until brown, then turning it, fat and all, into the shrimp pilau at the beginning of its cooking. The proportions are one cup of peeled, uncooked shrimps to one-half cup of washed, uncooked rice and two cups of boiling water. Salt and pepper to taste. Blend all ingredients, stirring until they begin to boil, then reduce heat and do not stir again. Cook twenty-five minutes, or until rice is tender and shrimps are a deep pink.

Shrimp and okra pilau is good. Most Floridians make this by adding pods of okra, sliced, to original mixture. I prefer to brown the okra slices in butter and add them to the pilau five minutes before it is done. A minced onion may be added to shrimp or shrimp and okra pilau, browning it with the bacon. Tomatoes may also be added. Both of these ingredients, while appealing to many tastes, to me destroy the delicate flavor of the shrimps.

Mutton Pilau

Rural Floridians do not make this, but I am partial to it. It must be similar to the original pilaf of Turkey, Persia and other Oriental countries where there are flocks of sheep. I make it like pork and chicken pilau, using enough mutton fat with the meat so that the pilau will be rich and oily.

Croquettes – Lamb, Ham, Chicken or Turkey

There is little excuse for wearing out the patience of a family by serving left-over meat plain cold sliced, day after day, when croquettes are so simple to make, and so tasty. I use the same recipe for left-over lamb, ham, chicken or turkey. Left-over beef is best made into stew, hash or pot-pie.

2 cups cold meat, put through grinder
2 tablespoons butter
3 tablespoons flour
1 cup milk
Salt and pepper to taste
2 tablespoons parsley
2 teaspoons Worcestershire sauce

Make a thick cream sauce of the butter, flour, milk and salt and pepper. Blend while hot with the ground meat and chopped parsley. Add the Worcestershire. Let chill. Mould into croquettes. Chill again. Dip in beaten egg, then in fine bread crumbs, and fry in croquette basket in deep smoking hot fat until a rich brown. These proportions serve three to four.

Stuffed Peppers

This is also a most acceptable way of using up the last bits of lamb, ham or beef. Make a cream sauce of two tablespoons butter, two tablespoons flour, one cup milk, salt and pepper to taste, for every two cups of ground meat. Add chopped parsley and a little Worcestershire sauce if desired. Parboil whole green peppers with the tops sliced off and the seeds and white membranes removed, ten minutes in boiling salted water. Stuff with mixture, allowing one-quarter cup to each pepper. Cover thickly with bread crumbs, dot with butter and bake in a hot oven until brown.

Minced Lamb

The very last of roast lamb, leg or shoulder, is very good served as minced lamb, especially when some of the brown lamb gravy is left. Put left-over lamb through the meat grinder with a few sprigs of parsley. Add to left-over gravy, add milk and a little flour thickening if necessary, one tablespoon butter, more salt if needed, and heat to boiling. Serve on toast. The mixture should be rather wet, but not runny.

Ground Liver for Sandwiches

Put left-over fried, broiled or baked liver through the meat-grinder. Blend one tablespoon cream and one tablespoon mayonnaise with every half-cup of the ground liver and use as a sandwich spread.

Beef Loaf

1¼ cups round steak and
¾ lb. fresh pork, ground together
1 egg
½ cup stale bread crumbs soaked in water
Salt, pepper
2 tablespoons minced parsley
Serves 6 to 8

Mix together, shape into a loaf, and bake in a buttered pan in which is placed one-half inch of boiling water. Bake one and one-half hours in a moderate oven. Beef loaf is also very good baked with one large can of tomatoes and one large sliced onion placed over and around it, basting the loaf from time to time with the sauce.

White Bacon with New Potatoes, Cream and Gravy

In Grandma's inexhaustible cellar there stood a crock of what she called pickled pork. This was a salt pork in a liquid brine. It was run-of-the-mill food to Grandma, but to her young visitor it was an immense treat. For it was served, fried to a succulent sweet crispness, with new potatoes and cream gravy. I got hungry for the remembered dish in an early day at the Creek, eyed the Florida white bacon, and decided it was worth trying. It worked. The white bacon did not have the peculiarly sweet flavor of the home-pickled pork, but the rest was the same.

Slice white bacon, or salt pork, in quarter-inch slices. Soak in warm water for ten minutes. Squeeze out, dip in flour and fry in an iron skillet until crisp and brown. Drain and keep hot. Turn out all but two tablespoons of the fat, and to the two tablespoons add one and one-half tablespoons flour. Stir until browned. Add one cup milk, salt and pepper to taste. Pour over new potatoes that have been scraped and boiled until tender. Dot the dish of potatoes and cream gravy with butter to make little golden pools. Serve with the crisp bacon.

Salads

A salad serves three purposes. Its noblest is as the one side dish when some hearty dish is served as the complete meal. It is also used as a filler when the meal is rather scanty. This too is commendable. It is also served for its nuisance value with a long, formal, or extremely hearty meal. This gives the diners a chance to catch their breath but has otherwise little use. I have often had guests struggle through a salad after a large dinner, only to be unable to eat some delectable dessert. For this reason, I am likely to serve celery hearts, strips of raw carrots, spring onions, along with the meat course and to dispense with the salad; or else to have the salad so light—a mere refreshing fragment of crisp lettuce, endives, water cress, with minced chives and French dressing—that no damage is done to my dessert.

I like a good salad particularly with a luncheon or supper dish. Any good cook book is full of salad recipes. I list only my own favorites.

Hawaiian Salad

Split small whole unpeeled pineapples in two, lengthwise, leaving leaves undisturbed. Allow one-half pineapple per person. Scoop out flesh and cut in small pieces. Add equal parts of cut orange and/or grapefruit sections and seedless or seeded white grapes, half a part of cut canned pears, bananas, and pitted Queen Anne cherries. Let fruit chill together in ice box. When ready to serve, drain well and fill chilled pineapple shells. Place a spoonful of mayonnaise and a Maraschino cherry on top of each portion, or dress with lime juice instead. This makes a complete hot-weather luncheon, served with cream-cheese sandwiches, an iced drink and a dessert.

For a high-vitamin, low-calorie luncheon for the plump, it is excellent, making the mayonnaise of mineral oil instead of ordinary salad oil, or dressing with lime juice, and serving with crisp soy-bean crackers.

Gingered Pear Salad

Mash a five-cent box of ginger snaps with a fork. Blend with one package of cream cheese until a smooth paste. Add a spoonful of heavy cream if mixture seems too dry.

Mound chilled pear halves with mixture. Serve on crisp lettuce leaves, with or without mayonnaise. The flavor is elusive, indefinable and very good.

Stuffed Tomato Salad

Choose medium-sized, ripe but firm tomatoes. Slice off stem end and scoop out flesh. Fill with a mixture, one-third to one-half cup to each tomato according to size.

> 1½ cup Cottage cheese
> 1 finely cut green pepper
> 1 medium-sized onion, minced
> ½ cucumber, diced small
> Top with a teaspoon of stiff mayonnaise

The unused tomato centers may be utilized in soup, or stewed with a few grains of salt and a little butter.

Tomato Aspic and Artichoke

> 1 14-oz. can tomato juice
> 1 envelope Knox plain gelatine
> 1 tablespoon lemon juice
> ⅛ teaspoon salt
> Few drops Worcestershire sauce
> 1 small can hearts of artichokes

Dissolve gelatine in three tablespoons of the cold tomato juice. Heat one cup of the tomato juice just short of boiling. Stir into soaked gelatine until blended. Add remaining cold tomato juice. Add lemon juice, salt and Worcestershire. Place an artichoke heart in the bottom of each individual mould and pour over it the mixture. Set in the ice box until firm. Serve on crisp lettuce with lemon-mayonnaise. Serves four.

The tomato mixture is a good base for any combination one wishes. Chopped celery, diced cucumber and a little onion juice is good. Also finely shaved raw carrots and finely broken nut meats.

Jellied Cabbage Salad

1 package lemon Jello
2 cups boiling water
1 tablespoon cider vinegar
⅛ teaspoon salt
1 cup grated cabbage
½ green pepper, finely cut
1 tablespoon grated horseradish
Serves 6

Dissolve Jello in boiling water. Let stand until cool but not set. Stir in remaining ingredients. Dip into individual moulds. Chill until firm. Serve on lettuce or endive with tart mayonnaise. This is especially good served, not as a separate course, but to accompany meats, particularly roast beef or pot roast of beef, roast leg of lamb or mutton.

I am an addict of jellied salads, as they can be prepared well in advance and there is no last-minute fussing with preparations.

Picnic Potato Salad

This recipe is rather fussy, from the many ingredients, but is well worth the trouble as an improvement over ordinary potato salad, which is simply too much potato.

4 cups diced cold potatoes (that have been boiled with the skins on, then plunged a moment in cold water before cooling and skinning)
1 cup finely cut celery, including some of the finer leaves
2 large onions, finely cut
1 green pepper, finely cut
4 pimientos, cut
3 tablespoons parsley, not too finely cut
3 tablespoons juice from sweet gherkin pickles
Mix in 1 cup Aunt Luella's boiled salad dressing. Cover and let stand in ice box several hours, or while other picnic materials are being prepared
As late as possible, add
½ small bottle capers
1 small bottle stuffed olives, sliced thin
1 cup cucumber, diced
8 sweet gherkins, cut very small

Stir in one cup tart mayonnaise. Whether served in salad bowl or carried in picnic bowl, garnish top with a light sprinkling of paprika, narrow strips of pimiento forming a sunburst in center, and halves of hard-boiled eggs arranged around the edge. More salt and pepper may be needed for some tastes. This quantity serves at least twelve.

Aunt Luella's Boiled Salad Dressing

1 teaspoon mustard (dry)
1 teaspoon salt
1 teaspoon cornstarch
1 tablespoon sugar
⅓ cup vinegar
1 egg yolk
1 tablespoon milk

Mix into a paste the mustard, salt, sugar and cornstarch with the vinegar. Beat the egg and add one tablespoon milk. Pour the thin paste of dry ingredients and vinegar slowly into the egg. Cook in a double boiler until thick. When partly cool, thin as desired with salad oil or milk.

Avocado Salad

Avocado—alligator pear—is of so mild and bland a flavor that it needs a pick-up. This may be had in the simplest form by dressing the avocado segments with a very tart French dressing. The Cubans, who have strong tastes, sometimes serve halves of avocado, pitted but with the skin left on as a shell, and filled with finely chopped white onion and French dressing. My own favorite way is to fill the halves with grated cabbage, to which has been added one teaspoon minced onion for every serving, the cabbage and onion marinated with French dressing before filling the avocados.

I also sometimes make the tomato jelly previously described, chill it just short of stiffening, and fill the avocado halves with the mixture, then chill until firm. In this case, I add one table-spoon of onion juice to the tomato jelly. A small spoonful of tart mayonnaise may be served on the top of each portion. Ordinarily, mayonnaise is too rich to serve with avocado.

Stuffed Avocado Rings

Cut an avocado in half, crosswise. Remove pit. Peel carefully. Pack cavities tightly with one package cream cheese blended with one teaspoon heavy cream and one tablespoon onion juice. Chill. When ready to serve, slice off stuffed rings about one-third inch in thickness. This makes an effective and also delicious garnish around a platter of cold meats. Or it may be served alone as a salad, on lettuce, with French dressing. It makes an attractive salad to be passed on a platter, alternating with or surrounding stuffed tomatoes. Do not experiment with adding any chopped mixture to the cream cheese, as it is difficult at best to slice rings neatly. If served alone as a salad, chopped nuts and parsley, or chopped celery and cucumber, may be scattered over the top, but this is gilding the lily.

A wonderful avocado recipe that may be served as a salad on crisp lettuce, is even better as a first course, but I include it here.

Avocado Francis

> 2 cups diced avocados
> 1 cup very finely diced celery
> 1 tablespoon minced chives (very important)
> ¼ cup home-made mayonnaise
> ½ cup chili sauce
> Juice of ½ lemon
> Chopped bacon
> Serves 8 as an entrée, 6 as a salad

Mix all ingredients except bacon, handling with a light touch. Let chill a few minutes in cold part of ice box. Serve in cocktail or sherbet glasses, or on lettuce, for a salad, and over the top scatter, one teaspoon to the serving, the chopped bacon that has been sautéed until brown and drained. The flavor of this dish is exceptional.

Grapefruit and Avocado Salad

Arrange peeled segments of grapefruit and crescent-shaped slices of peeled avocado alternately on lettuce leaves. Dress with French dressing.

Jellied Grapefruit with Pecans

2 grapefruit
1 package lemon Jello
1 cup boiling water
1 cup grapefruit juice
6 tablespoons chopped or finely broken
    pecan meats
Serves 4 to 6

Dice segments of grapefruit and drain. Dissolve Jello in boiling water. Add grapefruit juice. Cool just short of firmness. Add grapefruit and pecans. Place in fancy mould or in individual moulds. Set in ice box to harden. An old recipe from Charleston, in *200 Years of Charleston Cooking,* gives much the same recipe, adding a little sugar and using blanched chopped almonds instead of pecans. The almonds would doubtless be a trifle more delicate, but with hundreds of pounds of pecans from my own trees at the Creek, I use them when any nut-meat is called for.

I also make a jellied salad from any Florida citrus juice with gelatine, adding lemon juice to orange or tangerine juice. Thinly sliced kumquats are an addition to any citrus salad. Grapefruit segments over which are scattered sliced kumquats, using a French dressing containing a little sugar, make a good, light salad. Small balls of cream cheese and pecan meats are attractive with any such salad.

Mixed Green Salad with Herbs

Cut loosely and toss together endive, water cress, and a sprin
kling of finely chopped parsley, marjoram and chives or shal
lots, dressed with French dressing made with tarragon vine
gar. Serve from a bowl, or on individual large lettuce leaves.

Beet and Cabbage Salad

    1 cup cooked diced beets
    ½ cup grated cabbage
    ⅓ cup Aunt Luella's boiled dressing
    Serves 4 to 6

Mother's Sunday Night Salad

It is possible that the fruit salad we begged Mother to mak
on Sunday nights, offering to pick out the nut meats as a brib
tasted so good because it was Mother's—and I was young
Nothing ever seems to take the place of certain childhood fa
vorite dishes. But the combination of fruits could not go wrong
This serves six to eight.

    1 cup finely diced tart apples of fine flavor
    1 cup diced pineapple
    4 oranges, the meat cut in pieces
    1 cup seeded Malaga grapes
    4 sliced bananas
    ½ cup celery
    1 cup broken nut meats

In Mother's firm handwriting I find, "hickory nut meats or pecans are a necessity to make a success."

Blend with Mother's Fruit Salad Dressing.

Mother's Fruit Salad Dressing

½ cup sugar (scant)
½ cup of water
1 egg
1 tablespoon flour
2 teaspoons butter

Put water, sugar and butter in a small pan to boil. Dissolve the flour in two tablespoons water, add to the unbeaten egg and beat smooth with a rotary egg beater. Add boiling syrup and cook over a low flame, stirring constantly, until smooth and thick. Cool. Add a little thick cream, about one-quarter cup, when ready to mix with the fruit salad. Serve whipped cream on top of the salad.

Desserts

Every good cook has a sheaf of fine dessert recipes. Every good cook book is full of them. Even the novice has usually some specialty that she can turn out, with labor and pride. I knew a bride, fresh from college, who made a perfect chocolate cake. She could not understand why her husband became querulous when she served chocolate cake day after day after day, usually after some light college dish such as Welsh rarebit.

I have no intention of giving a comprehensive list of desserts. I offer only my own specialties that I consider a little out of the ordinary, and over which friends at the Creek have proved enthusiastic. I myself have little taste for a rich dessert after a hearty meal. I like to sit down on a summer afternoon and eat a whole quart of Dora's ice cream. I like to sit by the open hearth-fire on a winter's day, about four in the afternoon, and eat a quarter of a devil's food cake, with a pot of tea or coffee. But "company" seldom refuses dessert, and I have been known to invite ten for dinner just because I was in the notion to make a cake.

The most superb cake I have ever eaten in my life was Mother's almond cake. It made its appearance spectacularly for the Embroidery Club, at Thanksgiving, and on my birthday, when I was allowed to choose my own dinner menu. One of the regrets of my life is that I did not procure the recipe while Mother was alive. With all the recipes, added in her handwriting, to my childish cook book, I cannot understand how I failed to have her write down the recipe for this confection that makes all other cakes seem like sawdust. It took a day for the making. The almonds must be shelled, soaked in boiling water, the skins removed, the meats laid on a towel over the old-fashioned floor radiator to dry and blanch. They were chopped fine by hand in a chopping bowl—no heresy of the meat chopper for Mother, when she was making something special. The cake, as white as a virgin's breast, as tender as a mother's heart, was made in four layers. I can taste it still. I have never, from memory, duplicated it. The closest I come is as follows:

Mother's Almond Cake

> ¾ cup butter
> 1½ cups sugar
> ½ cup milk
> 2½ cups sifted flour
> ½ teaspoon cream of tartar
> 3 teaspoons baking powder
> Whites 8 eggs
> 1 teaspoon almond extract
> ½ teaspoon rose extract

Cream butter and sugar together into a large bowl, until smooth and light. Mix and sift dry ingredients. Add flour mixture and milk alternately, beating with an over-and-over motion, never *stirring*. Add almond and rose extract, then whites of eggs beaten until stiff, folding in carefully but quickly. Bake about twenty to twenty-five minutes in a moderately hot oven, about three hundred and seventy-five to four hundred degrees. Only experience teaches such things. Turn out layers to cool. Put together with almond paste filling. Ice top and sides with boiled frosting.

Almond Paste Filling

> 1 cup sugar
> ⅓ cup water
> 1 egg white
> 10 grains cream of tartar
> ½ teaspoon almond extract
> ½ teaspoon rose extract
> 1 lb. shelled almonds, blanched
>   and finely chopped

Boil sugar and water until the syrup spins a thread. Pour slowly into the stiffly beaten egg white, to which has been added the cream of tartar while beating. Beat until thick, add extracts and chopped almonds. Spread between layers. Cover top and sides of cake with boiled frosting.

Boiled Frosting for Almond Cake

1½ cups sugar
½ cup water
Whites of 2 eggs
Tiny pinch cream of tartar
¼ teaspoon each almond and rose extract

Boil sugar and water until syrup spins a thread. Beat slowly into stiffly beaten egg whites and cream of tartar. When nearly stiff, add flavoring. Beat until thick and spread over top and sides of cake. Garnish top with whole blanched almonds, arranged in daisy patterns.

Orange Cake

¼ cup butter
1 cup sugar
2 eggs
¼ cup milk
¼ cup orange juice
1⅔ cups sifted flour
2½ teaspoons baking powder

Cream butter, add sugar gradually, eggs well beaten, milk and orange juice. Add flour mixed and sifted with baking powder. Bake in two or three layers. Place orange filling between layers. Cover with orange frosting.

Orange Filling

½ cup sugar
2½ tablespoons flour
Grated rind 1 orange
¼ cup orange juice
½ tablespoon lemon juice
1 egg slightly beaten
1 teaspoon butter

Mix ingredients in order given. Cook in double boiler until thick. Cool before spreading.

Orange Frosting

Grated rind 1 orange
1 teaspoon brandy
½ teaspoon lemon juice
2 tablespoons orange juice
Yolk 1 egg
Confectioners' sugar

Add grated rind to brandy and fruit juices. Add slowly to yolk of egg, slightly beaten. Beat in confectioners' sugar, about one to one and one-half cups, until thick enough to spread.

The tragedy of the recipe for Mother's watermelon cake is more complete, since more exasperating, than that of the recipe for her almond cake. I can remotely copy, if not duplicate, the almond cake. The watermelon cake is gone beyond recall. She made it at the tail end of the Victorian era, when objects were designed to imitate other objects and æsthetic delight was supposed to ensue. It was the era of pictures made with sea shells, of toothpick holders in the shape of diminutive pot-pots, of porcelain knickknacks in the form of unnatural and revolting animals.

There was no point in making a cake to give the illusion of a watermelon. The flavor justified it. And the awed comments, "Why, it looks just like a watermelon," must have rewarded Mother for the long time it took for its making. I shall never forget the first time I remember seeing and eating it. It was my fifth birthday. With the long view toward starting me early on a successful social career, all the members of my kindergarten class and certain selected juvenile neighbors, were invited to the party. The occasion was to depart from the custom of accepting gifts, and it was announced that every child would receive one. I have wondered if I was not popular and this was a bribe to assure attendance. I don't remember being unpopular, but children don't always know. The time was summer and games were played on the lawn. The moment came for the dispersing of the gifts. Father, an ardent amateur horticulturist, had planted a small very choice imported French pear tree. This was of a size whose slender limbs could all be reached by children of kindergarten age. The individual gifts had been wrapped in tissue paper and tied to the imported pear tree with silk ribbons. At the signal, the guests, who were supposed to approach demurely, one by one, and pluck a gift, shrieked like Comanches and rushed pell-mell for the tree. It was torn literally limb from limb, and the neighborhood fat boy, arriving last in the race, fell prone on all that was left, the slender trunk, and flattened it to the ground. Anything but ice cream and the watermelon cake would have been an anti-climax. These inspired respect in the savage eyes, and the only indecorous note over refreshments was the fat boy, who, not to be outdone this time, made a dive for the remaining watermelon cake after slices had been served, and crammed two handfuls in his maw.

The cake was a deep loaf cake. Its base was white, it was thickly streaked with watermelon-pink, and chocolate blobs were scattered through it to represent seeds. It was iced with pistachio frosting in a delicate green. This is the way the recipe reads in my child's cook book:

Watermelon Cake

> White part
> 1 cup sugar
> ⅓ cup butter
> ⅓ cup milk
> Whites of 3 eggs
>   ups flour
>   easpoons baking-p.
> Red part
> ½ cup sugar
> ¼ cup butter
> ¼ cup mi
> 1 cup fl
> ½ teaspoon
> Whites of 3 e

Florida cockroaches have eaten away both edges. But even if it was all there, it does not tell how much vegetable coloring is used for the "red part," how to blend both parts so that they do not run together, and of what the chocolate seeds consist. My guess is that a small portion of the "white part" was held out, and one square of melted bitter chocolate added to this. But this mixture would be heavier than the rest. What is to keep the "seeds" from settling ignominiously and unnaturally to the bottom?

My guess as to the missing ingredients is one and one-half cups flour and two and one-half teaspoons of baking powder for the white part, and one-half teaspoon of baking powder (it could not be soda, with sweet milk) and the whites, of course, of three eggs for the red part. The white and red parts must have been spread alternately in the deep loaf pan, and a tiny spot of the chocolate batter dropped here and there between layers. It is possible that the red part, and the "seeds," were all in the middle, with the white part as a top and bottom layer, but I remember the cake as "streakity." I have never had the courage to try to make it, fearing adult disappointment. If it is as good as I remember it, it is worth a trial by any curious cook.

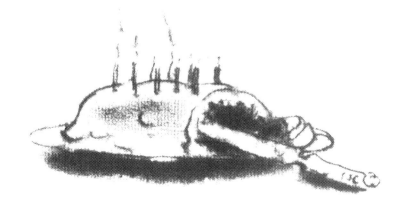

Aunt Theo's Cake

1 cup sugar, creamed with
½ cup butter
Drop in 2 eggs, beat
½ cup sour milk
1½ cups flour
¼ teaspoon salt
1 teaspoon grated nutmeg
1 teaspoon vanilla
1 teaspoon soda dissolved in
1 teaspoon water

Beat well. Bake slowly in a moderate oven in a loaf pan. Frost with thin layer of confectioner's frosting.

Devil's Food Cake

½ cup butter
½ cup white sugar
1½ cups brown sugar
4 egg yolks
1½ cups cake flour
¼ teaspoon baking powder
¼ teaspoon soda
¼ cup sour milk or buttermilk
4 oz. bitter chocolate
2 egg whites

Cream butter, stir in sugar gradually, and cream until light.

Add egg yolks and beat well. Add flour, sifted with baking powder and soda, alternately with milk. Stir in melted chocolate. Fold in stiffly beaten egg whites. Bake in three greased layer cake tins thirty to forty minutes, in a moderate oven (three hundred and fifty degrees). This is much moister than many devil's-food recipes. Frost with Seven Minute Frosting. (See page 158.)

Good Layer Cake

This is also one of Mother's recipes. I can vouch for it, as I make it when my game chickens are laying freely. From the ingredients, it *should* be good. It makes four layers.

> 1½ cups powdered sugar (not confectioners')
> 1 cup granulated sugar
> ¼ lb. of butter
> 1 cup milk
> 1½ pts. flour
> 3 teaspoons baking powder
> 5 eggs, yolks and whites beaten separately

Cream butter and sugar together until fluffy. Add beaten egg yolks. Fold in flour with baking powder, and milk, alternately. No flavoring is needed if a lemon or orange filling is used. If a chocolate or cocoanut or nut and raisin filling is used, flavor batter with one teaspoon vanilla.

Mother could be economical when necessary. I have from the first World War her recipe for eggless cake. It makes a very solid cake, but is moist and flavory and keeps well.

Seven Minute Frosting

2 egg whites, unbeaten
1½ cups sugar
5 tablespoons water
1½ teaspoons corn syrup
1 teaspoon vanilla

Put unbeaten egg whites, sugar, water and corn syrup in upper part of double boiler. Beat with rotary egg beater until sugar is dissolved. Place over boiling water, beating constantly with egg beater, and cook seven minutes, or until frosting will stand in peaks. Remove from fire. Add vanilla and beat until thick enough to spread.

Eggless Cake

1 cup brown sugar
½ cup lard (or Crisco) and butter
1 cup thick sour milk
½ cup raisins
½ cup currants
2 cups flour
1 teaspoon soda
1 teaspoon powdered cloves
1 teaspoon powdered cinnamon
½ teaspoon ground nutmeg

One cup of honey may be substituted for the brown sugar, in

which case reduce the sour milk to three-quarters cup. Cream sugar or honey with shortening. Stir in milk, then flour, and spices, saving out one-eighth cup of the flour to blend with the raisins and currants, now added. Dissolve soda in one teaspoon water and stir in. Beat very well. Bake about fifty minutes in a deep round tin or an angel-cake tin. Frost with boiled frosting or, if sugar is scarce, dust with powdered sugar. Nut meats may be added to the batter.

Black Chocolate Cake

½ cup shortening
½ cup brown sugar
¾ cup sour milk
2 eggs
2 squares chocolate, melted
2 cups flour
¾ teaspoon soda
¼ teaspoon salt
1 teaspoon vanilla

Mix ingredients in order, breaking in eggs whole and beating well. Soda is dissolved in one teaspoon water. Bake in moderate oven about forty-five to fifty minutes, in a square or rectangular pan. Frost with boiled or confectioner's frosting. This is an economical cake, but very good. To save sugar, if not expense, it is very good served cut in squares and topped with lightly sweetened whipped cream, instead of with frosting.

Mother's Washington Pie

⅔ cup sugar

2 eggs

1 cup flour, pinch of salt

1½ teaspoons baking powder

3 tablespoons rich sweet milk

Beat eggs very light. Add sugar gradually, beating, then milk gradually, beating well. Add flour, salt and baking powder sifted together. Bake in two layer tins. Fill and top with Cream Filling. This is of course a cake, not a pie. We never had it, certainly if company was present, without Father's joke. A gentleman called for Washington Pie in a restaurant and was served chocolate cake. "I wanted George Washington Pie," he said, "not Booker T." Mother always smiled wanly and dutifully. It is a very good light dessert.

Cream Filling

⅞ cup sugar

½ cup flour

⅛ teaspoon salt

2 eggs

2 cups scalded milk

1 teaspoon vanilla or ½ teaspoon
     lemon extract

Mix dry ingredients, add eggs slightly beaten, and pour on, slowly, and stirring constantly, scalded milk. Cook fifteen minutes in double boiler, stirring constantly until thickened, then occasionally. Cool and flavor. Do not add to so-called pie until both cake layers and filling are cold. It should be eaten within a few hours.

Any child who does not have a country grandmother who keeps a cooky jar is as much to be pitied as one who grows up with protruding teeth. If it is impossible for a grandmother to live in or move to the country, solely to insure the proper spiritual start for coming generations, at least it is possible to have a cooky jar. In Grandmother Traphagen's Michigan farmhouse, the two cooky jars stood on a shelf just inside the door that led from the kitchen down to the cellar. One left a divine odor behind, on opening the door, for the kitchen itself was always sweetly redolent, and in a cupboard in the dining room adjoining stood always a plate of raspberry tarts and deep soup plates of comb-honey, both clover and buckwheat. The fragrance of these is past description. But the opening of the cellar door sent a wave of compensation. In the cellar stood the wooden churn into which, night and morning, was skimmed inch-thick yellow cream from the broad shallow pans of milk. Butter was churned when the cream was scarcely turned and had a unique and delicious odor. Crocks of every sort of pickles and relish, of preserved or brandied peaches, pears and plums, of apple butter and peach butter, stood on the cold stone floor and gave off a thin cool scent of mingled spices. And on the shelves just inside the cellar landing, were the cooky jars—sugar cookies, molasses cookies, hickory-nut cookies. There was usually, too, an old-fashioned high-stemmed covered glass cake plate or two, holding what was strangely left of the previous meal's nut cake, jelly roll or blackberry-jam layer cake. From under the covers came the delectable smells. With permission, only as a technicality and a sop to adult authority, the grandchildren were allowed to "piece" on any of these or on the raspberry tarts. Mother did not believe in food between meals for children, but it was Grandma's house, and since she had successfully raised seven children on the theory that one should have food when one was hungry, we had free play. We very nearly always chose the cookies for the "piecing." Perhaps we had learned that consumption of the richer cakes and tarts spoiled our appetites for the coming incredible meal. Children are no fools, as modern pediatrics is discovering.

Grandma Traphagen's Sugar Cookies

2 cups sugar
1 cup butter (no substitute)
3 eggs
1 cup flour
¼ teaspoon soda dissolved in
3 tablespoons hot water

Cream butter and sugar together until light and fluffy. Add eggs, well beaten, then flour, then soda dissolved in hot water. Add enough more sifted flour to handle and roll out—not a flake more than is necessary. Cut in rather large rounds, about three inches across. Place on buttered cooky sheet and bake in hot oven (four hundred and twenty-five to four hundred and fifty degrees) about twelve minutes, or until golden brown. They must not be too brown. They are rich, of course, crisp when fresh, inclined to a delectable chewiness after standing.

Grandma Traphagen's Molasses Cookies

1½ cups granulated sugar
1 cup shortening
1 egg
1 cup molasses
1 cup buttermilk or sour milk
4 teaspoons soda
1 teaspoon salt
2 tablespoons vinegar
1 teaspoon cinnamon
½ teaspoon ginger
About 4 cups flour

Cream together the sugar and shortening. Break in the egg and beat vigorously. Add the molasses, salt, cinnamon and ginger and beat well again. Add the milk, then the soda dissolved in the vinegar, then the flour, using enough only to roll out well. Cut into large cookies and bake in a moderate oven on a greased sheet about twelve minutes. These are rather soft and very good. These proportions make a large family batch.

Ginger Snaps

1 cup butter (or Crisco)
1 cup molasses
1 cup sugar
1 tablespoon ginger
1 teaspoon soda
Flour, as much as can be worked in

Mix as for molasses cookies. Roll a piece the size of a marble in the hands, place on flat pans a little distance apart to allow for spreading. Bake in a moderate oven, about four hundred degrees, for ten to twelve minutes. Let them remain in pans until cool.

Aunt Flo's Molasses Cookies

These are not as good as Grandma's molasses cookies and Aunt Flo was allowed to make them only when Grandma was off gallivanting. I include Aunt Flo's recipe because it is extremely economical and sugarless (not that that aspect entered into it in her day) and makes healthy and substantial cookies eminently suitable for feeding hungry children between meals.

> 1 cup molasses
> 1 cup shortening (Crisco)
> 1 egg
> 1 tablespoon ginger
> 1 teaspoon cinnamon
> 1 teaspoon soda
> ½ cup boiling water
> 1 cup flour

Heat molasses slightly and beat in shortening, stirring until blended and cool. Stir in beaten egg. Add one cup flour. Add soda dissolved in boiling water. Add enough more flour to roll out well. Be careful, not to add too much flour, or cookies will be dry and tough. Roll out to one-quarter inch thickness. Cut into fairly large rounds, about three inches across. Bake on greased cooky sheet about twelve to fifteen minutes in a moderate oven (three hundred and fifty degrees).

Boston Brownies

1 cup sugar
⅓ cup butter
2 eggs
1 scant cup flour
½ cup raisins
1 teaspoon baking powder
2 squares melted chocolate in
¼ cup water
1 cup nut meats
½ teaspoon vanilla

Mix as for cake. Drop by spoonfuls on waxed paper laid in shallow pan. Bake in slow oven (three hundred and fifty degrees) about ten minutes.

Overnight Cookies

1 cup brown sugar
¼ cup butter
1 egg
⅛ teaspoon salt
1½ cups flour sifted with
½ teaspoon soda
¼ teaspoon cream of tartar
Dash nutmeg, cinnamon, vanilla

Knead and form into roll. A little more flour may be needed to make a stiff roll. Let stand overnight in ice box, or until ready to bake. Slice thin. Bake ten to twelve minutes in a moderate oven.

Date Cookies

1 cup sugar
⅔ cup shortening
2 eggs
4 tablespoons hot water
1 teaspoon soda
2 cups flour
¼ teaspoon salt
1 cup nut meats
1 lb. dates, cut up
½ teaspoon each clove, cinnamon

Cream butter and shortening. Add beaten eggs, then flour and salt, sifted, and soda dissolved in hot water. Add nut meats and dates, lightly dusted with flour. Bake in moderate oven.

Date Torte

Mix
1 cup sugar
2 tablespoons flour
1 teaspoon baking powder
Then
1 cup pitted and cut-up dates
1 cup nut meats
Last
2 eggs, well beaten

Spread in shallow pan to depth of about three-quarters inch. Sprinkle with powdered cinnamon. Bake thirty to forty minutes in a slow oven. Cut in squares and top generously with unsweetened whipped cream. This is very rich and mighty good.

Pecan Cream Torte

3 cups finely chopped pecans
1½ cups granulated sugar
6 eggs
2 tablespoons flour
2 teaspoons baking powder

Beat egg yolks well, add sugar gradually and beat until fluffy. Sift baking powder with flour, and mix with chopped pecans. Beat egg whites until stiff. Fold the flour and pecan mixture into the beaten egg whites. Then fold mixture lightly into egg yolks and sugar. Blend gently. Pour either into two layer cake tins or into a shallow rectangular pan, lined with greased paper. Bake fifteen to twenty minutes in a moderate oven, about three hundred and seventy-five degrees. Cool in pans. Just before serving, spread with sweetened whipped cream between and on top of layers, or on top of cut squares. Like the date torte, this is very rich.

Orange Sauce

One cup of pulverized sugar dissolved with juice of one-half orange and grated rind of one-half orange. Just before serving add one-quarter cup cream. Quantity may be increased by using juice of one orange and one-half cup cream.

Evadne's Gingerbread

> 3 eggs
> 1 cup sugar
> 1 cup molasses
> 1 teaspoon each of powdered
>   clove, ginger and cinnamon
> 1 cup Wesson oil

Place all above ingredients together in large bowl and beat well. Dissolve two level teaspoons soda in one-eighth cup hot water. Add to beaten mixture. Sift in two cups flour. Beat well. Add one cup boiling water and beat lightly and quickly. Pour into rectangular pan and bake forty-five minutes in a moderate oven. This batter will seem incredibly thin. Do not make the mistake of adding any more flour. It bakes into the most delicate and delicious gingerbread I have ever eaten. Serve hot in squares and top with generous mounds of unsweetened whipped cream.

Mother's Orange Pudding

> 1 pint milk
> ⅔ pint bread crumbs (rather coarse)
> 1 beaten egg
> 3 tablespoons sugar
> Pinch of salt

Soak milk and bread crumbs together about an hour. Beat egg and add sugar gradually, beating until fluffy. Add juice of one-half orange to egg and sugar and pinch of salt. Stir into soaked milk and crumbs. Turn into buttered glass baking dish and bake slowly until set and light brown on top. Cover with marshmallows and return to oven until marshmallows are puffed and golden brown. Serve immediately with orange sauce.

Apple or Peach Dumpling

Sift together one and one-half cups flour, one-eighth teaspoon salt and one and one-half teaspoons baking powder. Work in coarsely with fingers one and one-half tablespoons butter. Add about one-half cup milk, or just enough to hold mixture together. Too much milk toughens the dumplings. Roll out on a floured board into a sheet about one-half inch thick. Cut the dough into squares about four inches each way, or large enough to hold several thin slices of tart apples or well-flavored fresh peaches. Moisten edges of dough and fold, pinching edges tightly together to form a sealed case. If apples are very sour sprinkle a little sugar over them. Use no sugar for peaches. Place dumplings in a buttered shallow pan, buttering sides of dumplings so that they will not stick together. Place boiling water in pan to depth of one-quarter inch. Bake uncovered in moderate oven until crust is brown—but not too brown. Serve hot, preferably with generous quantities of sweetened thin cream, flavored with powdered cinnamon. A hard sauce is also good, but the sweetened cinnamon cream is far and away my favorite.

Steamed Pudding or Roly–Poly

2 cups flour
5 teaspoons baking powder
½ teaspoon salt
2 tablespoons butter
¾ cup milk
Fruit

Mix and sift dry ingredients. Work in butter with tips of fingers. Add milk gradually, cutting it in with a knife. Roll out. For apple pudding, place four sliced tart apples in middle of dough. Sprinkle with one tablespoon sugar, one-eighth teaspoon nutmeg, pinch of salt and dot with one-half teaspoon butter. Bring dough around apples and lift carefully into a buttered mould or deep round pan. Place in steamer over hot water, cover closely, and steam one hour and twenty minutes.

To make roly-poly, spread rolled-out dough thickly to within one-half inch of edge with black currant jam, blackberry or raspberry jam, gooseberry jam, sour orange marmalade, or with more thinly sliced apples or sliced peaches. Roll up like a jelly roll and place in buttered pan in steamer with the open edge down.

Steamed fresh blueberry or fresh blackberry pudding is made by increasing the quantity of milk in the dough to one cup instead of three-quarters, and sifting one-quarter cup more of flour over one and one-half cups berries, folding in berries to dough when mixed. Turn into round deep buttered pan and steam one hour and twenty minutes.

With any of the steamed puddings or roly-polies I prefer the sauce of sweetened cinnamon cream. Hard sauce is good with black currant roly-poly. Lemon sauce is good with steamed apple pudding.

Lemon Sauce

1½ cups boiling water
¾ cups sugar
2 tablespoons cornstarch
2 tablespoons butter
2 tablespoons lemon juice

Mix cornstarch and sugar in sauce-pan and pour on boiling water, stirring constantly. Place over very low fire and cook, stirring, until clear. Simmer four minutes. Add butter and lemon juice. Serve hot. A grating of nutmeg may be added if desired. This is also a good sauce to serve with a plain bread pudding.

Rice and Pineapple Pudding

1 cup boiled rice, well chilled
¼ cup sugar
1 cup shredded pineapple, chilled
1 cup whipped cream
⅛ teaspoon salt
½ teaspoon vanilla

With a fork, mix rice with sugar and salt and vanilla. Stir in pineapple. Add whipped cream lightly and quickly. Chill a few minutes and mound in sherbet glasses to serve. A Maraschino cherry or a cube of pineapple is attractive on top.

Baba au Rhum

This is a delicious cake dessert, very simple to make in spite of its elegant connotation of expensive restaurants. In this recipe, the cakes are less rich than most of the French ones, the sauce richer and, I think, better. The batter for the cakes must be handled with all possible speed when adding the flour and the hot milk, and no time must be lost in getting it into the very hot oven.

Cakes

2 eggs
1 cup sugar
1 cup flour
⅛ teaspoon salt
1 teaspoon baking powder
½ cup hot milk, just short of boiling
1 tablespoon butter

Beat eggs well. Add sugar slowly and beat until light and fluffy. Sift flour, salt and baking powder and fold quickly into egg and sugar mixture. Have butter melted in hot milk and pour into batter, blending rapidly with no more beating than necessary for mixing. Dip quickly by spoonfuls into greased small muffin tins—regular muffin tins will do, but the smaller cakes are more attractive—and bake about twenty minutes in a moderate oven, three hundred and seventy-five degrees. Turn out of tins and cool.

I serve this dessert at the table, probably because my old Shef-field double serving dish is perfect for the purpose. In one side of the server are the cakes. In the other side, the rum sauce, which I serve hot. I place a cake on an individual dessert plate and ladle several spoonfuls of the hot rum sauce over it. I work fast, as the cakes should not stand any longer than necessary in the sauce.

Hot Rum Sauce

> 1 cup brown sugar
> 1 cup granulated sugar
> 1 cup cold water
> 1½ tablespoons butter
> ⅜ cup rum (I prefer Puerto Rico rum
> —Jamaica is a little too strong)

Bring sugar and water to boil. Let boil three minutes. Remove from fire and add butter. Let cool thirty seconds. Add rum. To conserve sugar, one cup honey and one-quarter cup each of brown and white sugar may be used.

Black Bottom Pie

I think this is the most delicious pie I have ever eaten. The recipe from which I first made it was sent me by a generous correspondent, and originated at an old hotel in Louisiana. It seemed to me it could be no better. Then another correspondent sent me a recipe for Black Bottom Pie that varied in some de-tails from the first one. Having tried both, I now combine the two to make a pie so delicate, so luscious, that I hope to be propped up on my dying bed and fed a generous portion. Then I think that I should refuse outright to die, for life would be too good to relinquish. The pie seems fussy to make, but once a cook gets the hang of it, it goes easily.

Crust

14 crisp ginger cookies
5 tablespoons melted butter

Roll out the cookies fine. Mix with the melted butter. Line a nine-inch pie tin, sides and bottom, with the buttered crumbs, pressing flat and firm. Bake ten minutes in a slow oven to set.

Basic Filling

1¾ cups milk
1 tablespoon cornstarch
4 tablespoons cold water
1 tablespoon gelatine
½ cup sugar
4 egg yolks
Pinch of salt

For Chocolate Layer

2 squares melted chocolate
1 teaspoon vanilla

For Rum-Flavored Layer

4 egg whites
⅛ teaspoon cream of tartar
½ cup sugar
1 tablespoon rum

Topping

2 tablespoons confectioners' sugar
1 cup whipping cream
Grated chocolate

Soak the gelatine in the cold water. Scald the milk, add one-half cup sugar mixed with the cornstarch, pinch of salt, then beaten egg yolks. Cook in double boiler, stirring constantly, until custard thickens and will coat the back of the spoon. Stir in the dissolved gelatine. Divide custard in half.

To one-half add the melted chocolate and the vanilla. Turn while hot into the cooled crust, dipping out carefully so as not to disturb crust.

Let the remaining half of the custard cool. Beat the egg whites and cream of tartar, adding one-half cup of sugar slowly. Blend with the cooled custard. Add one tablespoon rum. Spread carefully over the chocolate layer. Place in ice box to chill thoroughly. It may even stand over-night. When ready to serve, whip the heavy cream stiff, adding two tablespoons confectioners' sugar slowly. Pile over the top of the pie. Sprinkle with grated bitter or semi-sweet chocolate.

Chocolate Pie

After once tasting Black Bottom Pie, any ordinary chocolate pie seems a poor substitute. But since there are times when one does not want to take either the time or the expensive ingredients to make the former, here is a very good, quick and inexpensive chocolate pie recipe.

½ cup sugar
4 tablespoons flour
1 cup milk
5 tablespoons cocoa
⅛ teaspoon salt
2 egg yolks
½ teaspoon vanilla

Scald the milk in the top of a double boiler. Mix well together the sugar, cocoa, flour and salt and add to the milk. Stir in the beaten egg yolks and cook, stirring constantly, until the mixture is well thickened. Remove from fire, cool slightly, and add the vanilla. Chill, and turn into a crisp baked pie crust. Top with meringue made of two egg whites beaten stiff, to which is added slowly four tablespoons powdered sugar and one-half teaspoon vanilla. Place eight minutes in a slow oven for meringue to brown.

Orange Chiffon Pie

Follow lemon chiffon pie recipe, using a scant half-cup of orange juice and one tablespoon lemon juice instead of the half-cup of lemon juice, and substituting grated orange rind for lemon rind.

Chef Huston's Lemon Chiffon Pie

Place in top of double boiler
3 egg yolks slightly beaten
½ cup sugar
⅙ teaspoon salt
Stir constantly until thickened
Add to hot custard
**1 tablespoon gelatine that has been
    soaked in**
½ cup cold water
Stir until dissolved and add
½ cup lemon juice
1 teaspoon grated lemon rind
Cool the custard

Beat stiff three egg whites, adding slowly one-half cup sugar. Fold into the cooled custard. Turn into a crisp baked pie crust or into tart shells. Chill. Top with rosettes of whipped cream.

Lime Chiffon Pie

Follow recipe for lemon chiffon pie, using fresh lime juice instead of lemon juice, and only one-half teaspoon grated lime rind. This makes a delicious tropical dessert of an exquisite pale green.

Strawberry Chiffon Pie

I hold fresh strawberries in such respect that this very dainty pie seems to me something of a sacrilege. Yet I strain strawberries to make Dora's fresh strawberry ice cream, so should not balk at doing the same to make a fancy party pie.

Cut very small one quart fresh (or frozen) washed and hulled strawberries. Cover with one-quarter cup sugar and let stand several hours. Strain through cheesecloth. Soak four tablespoons gelatine in one-third of the juice. When dissolved, add one tablespoon lemon juice and add to remainder of strawberry juice, stirring well until gelatine is blended. Cool mixture in ice box but do not allow to stiffen. Add a few grains of salt and two-thirds cup sugar to six unbeaten egg whites and heat in top of double boiler over hot water until barely lukewarm. Remove from hot water and beat stiff with a rotary egg beater. Fold into the strawberry mixture. Turn into a baked crisp pie shell and chill until firm. When ready to serve, cover with whipped cream, to which is added two tablespoons confectioners' sugar and one-quarter teaspoon lemon juice.

Banana Cream Pie

Make a stiff boiled custard of one pint milk, three egg yolks, one-half cup sugar, pinch of salt and three tablespoons cornstarch. Cool and add one teaspoon vanilla. Chill. In a crisp baked pie crust place a layer of sliced bananas, a layer of custard, then bananas, until custard is used. Cover with a layer of slightly sweetened whipped cream. Serve very cold.

Butterscotch Pie

This is an old country-woman's recipe, and she spells vanilla "Vamallia." It is inexpensive and good and not unduly rich.

> 1 cup brown sugar
> 1 cup water
> 1½ teaspoons butter
> Yolk of 1 egg
> 2 tablespoons flour
> 4 tablespoons cream
> ½ teaspoon "Vamallia"

Put on sugar, water and butter to boil. Beat the egg yolk until light and add the cream, in which has been well blended the flour. Stir into the syrup that has been boiling three minutes. Turn flame very low and cook until thick, stirring constantly. Remove from fire and add vanilla. Beat one or two egg whites stiff and stir into the hot mixture. Cool slightly and turn into a baked pie crust. If desired, a meringue may go on top, or whipped cream. The last direction is simple and very much to the point. The old lady wrote:

> then Eeat.

Pecan Pie

True Southern pecan pie is one of the richest, most deadly desserts of my knowledge. It is more overpowering than English treacle pie, which it resembles in texture, for to the insult of the cooked-down syrup is added the injury of the rich pecan meats. It is a favorite with folk who have a sweet tooth, and fat men in particular are addicted to it.

Utterly Deadly Southern Pecan Pie

> 4 eggs
> 1¼ cups Southern cane syrup
> 1½ cups broken pecan meats
> 1 cup sugar
> 4 tablespoons butter
> 1 teaspoon vanilla

Boil sugar and syrup together two or three minutes. Beat eggs not too stiff, pour in slowly the hot syrup, add the butter, vanilla and the pecan meats, broken rather coarsely. Turn into a raw pie shell and bake in a moderate oven about forty-five minutes, or until set.

My Reasonable Pecan Pie

I have nibbled at the Utterly Deadly Southern Pecan Pie, and have served it to those in whose welfare I took no interest, but being inclined to plumpness, and having as well a desire to see out my days on earth, I have never eaten a full portion.

I do make a pecan pie that is not a confection, like the other, not as good, if one is all set for a confection, but that I consider very pleasing and definitely reasonable.

Make a thick custard as for Banana Cream Pie, using brown sugar instead of white, and adding two tablespoons butter. Chill the custard, add one cup coarsely broken pecan meats, one tea-spoon vanilla, and turn into a baked crisp pie crust. Top with sweetened whipped cream. Dear knows, this is deadly enough.

Loquat Pie

Line a pie tin with crust. Fill with peeled and seeded loquats. If loquats are dead ripe, sprinkle over one-half cup sugar. If they are not extremely ripe, increase the sugar to nearly one cup. Sprinkle over one tablespoon lemon juice if loquats are very ripe. Sift over one tablespoon flour. Dot with butter. Make a strip-top open crust and bake about forty-five minutes.

Strawberry Shortcake

2 cups flour
¼ cup sugar
4 teaspoons baking powder
½ teaspoon salt
Few grains of nutmeg (important)
1 egg
⅓ cup butter
⅓ cup milk

Mix dry ingredients and sift twice. Work in shortening with tips of fingers. Add egg well beaten, then milk. Turn without rolling into a well-buttered round tin and pat into shape with the flat of the hand. Bake about fifteen minutes in a hot oven.

An hour before ready, cut one quart fresh strawberries (one and one-half quarts are better) in quarters, saving out at least a dozen of the largest and choicest berries. To cut berries, add three-quarters cup brown sugar. Let stand in bowl in a warm place. The mixture should be warm when ready to serve. Split the shortcake, hot from the oven, into two layers. Butter each cut side. Keep buttered side up. Put layers together with strawberries and juice between and on top. Top with the choice whole berries and serve with whipped cream.

Pecan Souffle

> ¼ cup butter
> ¼ cup flour
> ½ teaspoon salt
> 1 cup milk
> 3 eggs yolks, well beaten
> ½ cup sugar
> 1 cup finely chopped pecan meats
> 1 teaspoon vanilla
> 3 egg whites, stiffly beaten

Melt butter in top of double boiler. Add flour and salt, mixing well. Add milk gradually, stirring constantly. Cook to make a thick paste. Combine well beaten egg yolks, sugar, pecans and vanilla, and mix well. Add to this the cooked butter and flour and milk mixture and stir until well blended. Fold the stiffly beaten egg whites carefully into this mixture. Turn into a buttered casserole. Place in a pan of hot water, to the depth of one and one-half inches. Bake in a moderate oven, three hundred and fifty degrees, from forty-five to sixty minutes, until set, or until silver knife blade comes out clean from the soufflé. Serve at once, passing a bowl of slightly sweetened whipped cream to which has been added one-half teaspoon grated lemon rind. Supposed to serve six, but four will eat it.

Peach Shortcake

Use the recipe for Mother's Biscuits. Cut into individual large biscuits, about three inches across. Bake in a hot oven about twelve minutes. Split, butter cut sides lightly, place between and on top of the joined layers fresh sliced peaches that have stood one-half hour in ice box in one-quarter cup sugar to every cup of peaches. Place a generous mound of unsweetened whipped cream on each shortcake.

I always keep on hand in the pantry cans of sliced or halves of peaches, and a good shortcake may be made on a moment's notice. I usually make enough dough to have biscuits with the meal, saving out enough to make the individual shortcakes for dessert.

Sweet Potato Pone

This is a dessert peculiar to the Deep South, and the ingredients vary according to what the household possesses. I remember the time my friend Moe accepted, somewhat to my distress, an invitation to a family Christmas dinner my first year in Florida. He made no comment as he made his way through the meal that had taken me days to prepare. I said to him, "This is a typical Yankee Christmas dinner. Now tell me, what is a typical Cracker Christmas dinner?" "Whatever we can git, Ma'am," said Moe. "Whatever we can git." Sweet potato pone is made according to whatever we can git.

The most rudimentary sweet potato pone is a thick, gelatinous pudding. Small fry among poor blacks and whites consider it a treat of treats. Old colored Martha makes this type by peeling and grating raw sweet potatoes. To two cups of the grated potato she adds two tablespoons flour, three tablespoons of grease from fried white bacon, one-half teaspoon soda, one cup of Florida cane syrup, and enough water to make a rather thin mixture. This is baked in a shallow pan in a slow oven until set and slightly browned. When Martha has eggs, she adds an egg or two. When she has milk, she uses milk instead of water. When "the chillen" are coming to visit, she uses butter instead of the bacon grease. On these occasions she may have cream to churn, and she chants:

"Come, butter, come.

Grandma waitin' for the chillen to come."

From this simple basic recipe, sweet potato pone graduates to an elegant recipe like this:

2½ cups raw grated sweet potatoes (yams)

1 cup molasses

2 eggs

2 cups rich milk

1 tablespoon melted butter

1 teaspoon ground ginger or grated
    orange rind

1 tablespoon brown sugar

½ teaspoon powdered cinnamon

Add the molasses, well-beaten eggs, milk, melted butter and ginger or orange rind, in order, to the grated potatoes. Turn into a well-greased baking pan and bake about forty-five minutes in a moderate oven, sprinkling the brown sugar and cinnamon over the top at the end of the first twenty-five minutes.

Persimmon Pone

The same recipe makes persimmon pone, using the pulp of either wild or Japanese persimmons instead of grated potato, and ginger always, instead of orange rind.

Cassava Pudding

I have never made this, since I have never had the cassava roots to work with. But I accept a piece whenever offered me off in the Big Scrub, where Mistress Piety raises the tall ornamental bushes in her sandy yard, digs the roots and makes the pudding. The roots are washed, scraped and grated. Part of the starch is washed out in cold water. The grated pulp is mixed with country cane syrup, an egg or two, and a spoonful of butter. It is baked like sweet potato pone. It becomes completely transparent, of a clear amber color, and has much the texture of gum drops. It is served cold or only warm, cut in squares.

Light Desserts

I am partial to serving rather light desserts, rather than rich cakes and pies and puddings, especially after a hearty meal. I make a good many gelatine desserts, for their lightness, their keeping qualities against unexpected company, and because it is extremely convenient to have them prepared well ahead of time.

Orange Jelly

> 1 tablespoon gelatine
> ¼ cup cold water
> ¼ cup boiling water
> 1¼ cup orange juice
> ¾ cup sugar (½ cup if oranges
>   are very sweet)
> 1½ tablespoons lemon juice

Let gelatine stand five minutes in cold water. Pour on boiling water and stir until dissolved. Stir in orange juice, lemon juice and sugar, blending well. Turn into individual moulds or sherbet glasses and chill until set. Serve plain, or with unsweetened whipped cream or plain thin cream.

Kumquat Jelly

> 1½ cups kumquat juice
> ½ cup sugar
> ¼ cup Sauterne (domestic will do)
> 1½ tablespoons Orange Curacao
> 1 tablespoon gelatine
> 2 tablespoons cold water
> Few grains salt

Wash about two cups kumquats, cut in slices, add cold water to cover, bring slowly to boiling point and simmer one-half hour. Strain. There should be one and one-half cups juice. Add sugar, Sauterne and Curaçao. Soak gelatine five minutes in cold water. Bring kumquat mixture just short of boiling point and pour over gelatine, stirring well. Add salt. Turn into fancy mould or into individual moulds or sherbet glasses. Serve with whipped cream or with halves of kumquats seeded, cooked in sugar syrup until soft, and drained, or both.

Coffee Jelly

I make this of left-over breakfast or dinner coffee. Use one tablespoon gelatine to every two cups of coffee, dissolving in two tablespoons of the cold coffee, heating one-half cup of the coffee to boiling and stirring into gelatine, adding the remaining cold coffee last and stirring. Either make jelly without sugar and serve with sweetened thin cream, or add two to three teaspoons sugar to the jelly and serve with unsweetened cream.

Jellied Pecans

1 tablespoon gelatine
¼ cup cold water
¼ cup boiling water
½ cup sugar
½ cup sherry (sweet)
½ cup orange juice
2 tablespoons lemon juice

Make as orange jelly, adding sherry last, after mixture has cooled a little. Cover bottom of square or rectangular shallow pan with half of the mixture. Place in ice box, keeping remainder in kitchen. When chilled portion is nearly set, cover with halves of pecans placed one inch apart. Cover with remaining jelly. Chill until firm. Cut in squares, so that a pecan is in each square. Top with mounds of whipped cream. Walnuts or almonds may of course be used in place of the pecans.

The recipe for grapefruit and pecan jelly, given under Salads, may also be served as a dessert, with sweetened whipped cream.

Ice Cream Mousse

Now and then I overestimate the capacity of guests for Dora's ice cream, and after they have had their fill, and Idella hers, and old colored Martha and old Will have had a dish, and even the dog a lick or two, there is still ice cream left. I remove this from the freezer, place it in the ice box, and the next morning make a delicious mousse. For two cups of whatever the ice cream may be, I add one and one-half tablespoons gelatine dissolved in two tablespoons cold water. I heat one-third cup of rich milk or thin cream, or of water, according to the nature of the ice cream, and stir this into the dissolved gelatine, then stir in the ice cream mixture and turn into sherbet glasses. Chill until set.

Macaroon Cream

1 tablespoon gelatine
¼ cup cold water
2 cups rich milk, scalded
3 eggs
⅓ cup sugar
⅔ cup crumbled macaroons
Pinch of salt
1 teaspoon vanilla

Make a custard of the milk, the yolks of the eggs, sugar and salt. Add to the gelatine soaked in the cold water. Place pan in ice water, stirring frequently. When partly cool, stir in the finely crumbled macaroons and the vanilla. Continue stirring until mixture is cold and thickened. Then add the whites of the eggs beaten stiff. Turn into a mould, chill thoroughly, and serve garnished with whole macaroons.

Orange Fluff

2 egg yolks
2 tablespoons sugar
Grated rind of ½ lemon
Grated rind of ½ orange
5 tablespoons orange juice
1 tablespoon lemon juice
1 tablespoon hot water

Combine ingredients in order, beating the egg yolks with the sugar. Cook in the top of a double boiler until the mixture coats the back of a spoon, stirring constantly. Beat two egg whites until stiff, with one tablespoon sugar. Blend lightly but thoroughly with the custard mixture while it is still hot. Turn into sherbet glasses. This is a delicate and healthful dessert for young children or invalids.

Italian Loaf

2 cups rich milk
⅔ cup sugar
6 eggs
Pinch of salt
2 tablespoons gelatine
½ cup cold water
⅔ cup seeded raisins
½ cup Maraschino cherries
    cut in halves
1 teaspoon vanilla
½ teaspoon almond extract

Make a custard in the double boiler of the milk, sugar, salt and the yolks of the eggs. This is one of Mother's recipes, and I have found that four eggs do almost as well, adding one tablespoon cornstarch in such a case. The loaf is not as fluffy but there is no difference in taste. When the custard is thick and will coat the back of the spoon, stir in the gelatine dissolved in the cold water and turn into a bowl standing in ice water. Add the raisins, Maraschino cherries, vanilla and almond extracts. I also like pineapple cut in small pieces (not shredded) in place of the raisins. Stir the mixture occasionally until it cools and thickens somewhat, keeping ice in the water around the bowl. Then add the whites of the eggs beaten stiff. Turn into a melon-shaped mould and chill thoroughly. Serve with slightly sweetened whipped cream.

Orange Cream Tapioca

3 cups rich milk
3 tablespoons Minute Tapioca
⅛ teaspoon salt
Orange sections
1 tablespoon cold water
2 eggs, separated
8 tablespoons sugar
1 tablespoon grated orange rind
1 tablespoon lemon juice

Scald milk in double boiler, add tapioca and salt and cook about five minutes, or until tapioca is transparent, stirring constantly. Add cold water to egg yolks and beat well. Add six tablespoons of the sugar, beating, and the grated orange rind. Add the tapioca mixture to this, return to double boiler and cook until it thickens and coats the back of the spoon. Add lemon juice and cool. Fold in the egg whites that have been beaten stiffly with the remaining two tablespoons sugar. Alternate two layers of mixture with two layers of orange sections (removing white membranes) and chill, preferably in glass dish in which it is to be served.

Syllabub

This is the Deep South dessert that is supposed to start Southern beaux and belles on their drunken downfall, since it is so mild that children are allowed to have it, thus acquiring a taste for

the flavor of all liquors. The idea is silly, and the syllabub is
delicious.

> 1 cup Dora's cream
> 1 egg white
> ½ cup powdered sugar
> 2 tablespoons sherry, Madeira or
>   brandy
> Fruit to taste

Whip the cream with one-quarter cup of the powdered sugar
until stiff. Beat the egg white stiffly with the other one-quarter
cup of sugar. Combine, mixing well but lightly. Add the wine
and pour over the fruit. There are several combinations that are
good: two sliced bananas and two oranges cut in small pieces;
one-half cup diced pineapple and two oranges or three tangerines cut in small pieces; one cup fresh peaches diced, and allowed to stand a few minutes with one tablespoon lemon juice
and two tablespoons powdered sugar. I have even made fig
syllabub, soaking one cup of fresh or cooked Florida sugar figs
cut small in two tablespoons brandy or sherry and two tablespoons powdered sugar. The combinations are endless. The
moral damage is negligible.

Floating Island

This is a healthful old stand-by among desserts. The name is
probably a trick for inducing children to eat a sensible dessert
and feel excited about it. It is simply a plain boiled custard made
of two cups milk scalded in the top of the double boiler, adding
the lightly beaten yolks of three eggs, mixed with one-half cup

sugar, a pinch of salt, stirring constantly until it thickens and will coat the back of the spoon. A teaspoonful of vanilla is added, the custard chilled, and served in a fancy bowl with floating islands on top made by beating the whites of three eggs stiff with two tablespoons powdered sugar, and dropping by the spoonful on top of the custard. A sprinkling of pink sugar crystals is attractive.

I use the custard often as an emergency dessert, serving it over any fruit available—orange sections, bananas, diced pineapple, or fresh peaches.

Orange Ice Box Cake

This is technically a cake, but is so light and delicate that I include it among the light desserts.

> **1 cup orange juice**
> **Grated rind of 1 orange**
> **3 eggs**
> **½ cup sugar**
> **1 tablespoon butter**
> **1 cup heavy cream**
> **1 tablespoon cornstarch**
> **2 sponge cake layers**

Blend the sugar and cornstarch, add well-beaten egg yolks, butter, orange juice and grated rind, and cook in double boiler until thick. Cool. Beat together the egg whites and the cream and add to the cooled custard. Split the sponge cake layers and spread the mixture between layers and over the cake. Let stand in ice box overnight or at least six hours.

Coeur Flotant

This is Floating Island in its opera clothes. Make a plain boiled custard, flavoring with one teaspoon lemon juice and a little grated lemon rind instead of with vanilla. Place about one-half cup of the chilled custard in each individual large sherbet glass or dessert dish. Place in the center a large spoonful of thin cream, sweetened and frozen in a hand freezer. Arrange sections of almost any fresh fruit around the frozen cream—peaches, mangos, finger strips of pineapple, bananas, strawberries, oranges or tangerines. Sprinkle with grated bitter chocolate. The combination of flavors and textures is well worth the extra trouble of freezing the cream.

Baked Guavas

Use large ripe guavas. Cut off the tops and scoop out enough of the center to hold one teaspoon sugar each. Bake in a hot oven with a small amount of water in the pan, until tender when pierced with a long-tined fork. Serve hot, covered with chilled boiled custard.

Guavas and Cream

For all their exquisite flavor, I cannot consider guavas a perfect fruit because of the seeds. They lie in obtrusive layers between the layers of flesh, like rows of buckshot. Folk with a passion for guavas eat the seeds along with the fruit, and make an intolerable racket. One may painstakingly remove the seeds before serving the fruit, but it is a labor of love. For a dessert guava, the finest is the canned Cuban guava. I have found these only in the Cuban quarter in Tampa. There are Florida canned guavas, but the seeds are left in and the syrup is not so heavy. The canned Cuban guavas served with thin cream, or eaten with cream cheese and crackers, make a ravishing light dessert.

Guava jelly, cream cheese and crackers make of course a standard dessert. It is a pity that our small tart Cattley guavas are not grown in commercial quantities, for the jelly made from these is infinitely superior to ordinary guava jelly.

Ambrosia

Make alternate layers of orange sections, fresh grated or canned shredded coconut, tangerine sections, finely chopped pecans and powdered sugar. Let stand in ice box one hour before serving.

Baked Sherried Grapefruit

This is a delicious light dessert, summer or winter. It is also a superlative first course for a course dinner. I use it, too, in place of a salad, or served along with a rich meat, such as duck, game, ham or chicken, as cranberry jelly is served with turkey. In winter, I sometimes serve it for a company breakfast, using less sugar and clove.

Cut grapefruit in halves and separate sections as for breakfast serving, but do not cut the sections quite through. Turn upside down to drain off excess juice. Sprinkle the edges with brown sugar, powdered clove and dots of butter. Fill the center with sherry. Bake under a broiler or preferably in a hot oven until lightly browned. Serve hot.

Fried Plantains

Plantains are a tropical member of the banana family, of firmer texture. I find them usually in Tampa, for they are a favorite dish among the Cubans. When ripe, they are completely black and look a little withered.

Peel and cut lengthwise in very thin slices. Sauté in an iron skillet in butter. Turn frequently, and every time the slices are turned, sprinkle with sugar. Serve hot and brown, and pour over the caramelized juice.

Fried plantains are also delicious served with fried chicken or ham.

Clotted Cream

Turn milk from the evening milking into a deep, narrow kettle holding about one gallon. Let stand in ice box overnight. In the morning, place far back, preferably on an old-fashioned wood stove. A tremendously low flame covered with an asbestos mat, on an ordinary stove, is possible but risky, as the milk must never become actually hot. The milk should stand for eight hours, undisturbed, over the lowest possible heat. By evening, or after eight hours, the cream may be lifted off in a solid layer. Place in a covered bowl in the ice box, and any time after the next morning it is ready to use. It will keep in a good box for two or three days.

Serve with fresh whole strawberries, raspberries, fresh sliced peaches, or with almost any rich preserves—pear, pear and pineapple, peach preserves or spiced or brandied peaches, plum preserves, canned apricots, etc. A small serving of the fruit or the preserves is placed on one side of the dessert plate, and a ladle of the clotted cream next to it but not over it.

Orange Fritters

Peel oranges and separate into sections. One orange makes fritters for two or three. Remove seeds, if any, carefully, making the smallest possible incision. Dip sections in batter made of

> 1 cup flour
> 1½ teaspoon baking powder
> 2 tablespoons powdered sugar
> ¼ teaspoon salt
> ⅓ cup milk
> 1 egg
> 1 tablespoon melted butter

Mix salt, flour, sugar and baking powder, add milk gradually, egg well beaten, and melted butter. Fry in deep hot fat.

Sprinkle fritters with powdered sugar, to which may be added, if desired, one-half teaspoon grated orange rind. Serve hot. Thin cream may be passed. The fritters are also good served as a vegetable with chicken, lamb, ham, duck or game. For this purpose, eliminate the sugar from the batter and do not sprinkle the fritters with sugar.

Figs and Cream

Almost every yard in rural Florida has its fig tree. It is usually the little sweet sugar fig variety. They ripen in August and it is a race against the mockingbirds, the red birds and the bluejays to gather the figs. They make a delicate dessert served whole with cream and sugar.

Papayas

A fresh, thoroughly ripened papaya bears no relation to the sickening sweet canned papaya juices. It must be so ripe that it is a mass of black spots, so that the uninitiated would think only that it was time to throw it out. The flavor is mild and needs the addition of lime juice, preferably, or lemon juice. The papaya is peeled and cut in small cubes. Sprinkle generously with Florida lime juice and let stand in the ice box at least an hour before serving. It is an acceptable dessert after a heavy meat particularly, as it is high in pepsin. The pellet-like black seeds are high in pepsin, too, and are sometimes served scattered over the papaya cubes. Diced papaya also makes a good first course, or a course to be served in sherbet glasses with the meat, as one would serve an ice.

Japanese Persimmons

These are delicious served with cream and sugar.

Mangos

When Captain Haden developed the Haden mango near Miami, he did a greater kindness to the state than the Plant or Flagler railroad systems. The texture is like cream melting on the tongue. The flavor is as though nightingales were singing to the palate. What the gods gorged on, on Olympus, is called nectar and ambrosia, but mangos are plainly meant. When ripe, the flesh yields slightly to the impatient finger and the jade-green skin turns the rose and yellow of a June sunset. I make fancy things with mangos (see Ice Creams), but when I am left to myself, I just shut the kitchen door, lean over the sink, peel the mango, cut off inch-thick slices and, as the old lady directed for her pie, "then Eeat." They are also superb sliced and served with sugar and cream, and on many a hot summer evening I have made a supper of a soup plate of the slices, dabbed with ladlefuls of Dora's thick golden cream from the morning's skimming. The bathroom scales are then turned to the wall for a few days.

Dora's Ice Cream

A Navy flier recently arrived in Hawaii, tormenting himself with the talk of food in *Cross Creek,* wrote, "You will be interested to know that the Hawaiian mangos are very good—and my, don't I wish I had Dora!"

I sometimes think that, as the supreme sacrifice, I might give Dora to my country. She is irreplaceable. Her mother, old Laura, gave cream almost as thick, and Dora's pretty heifer daughter Chrissie looks most promising, but Dora—and her cream—stand alone. She gives no great quantity of milk, her disposition is vile and we dislike each other, but I joyfully swap her the most expensive twenty-per-cent dairy feeds, and allow her to nibble on my coral honeysuckle and my oranges, and raise fine cow-pea hay for her, in return for her cream. It rises to a depth of three-quarters of an inch on a shallow pan of milk.

It is as yellow as buttercups. It is so thick, when ladled off into a bowl or pitcher, that it is impossible to pour. It must be spooned out. My friends rejoice with me in her possession. I cannot imagine living a life through, without a Dora.

On last Christmas Eve my wonderful pointer, Pat, was killed at the Creek by a speeding automobile. I set my teeth not to spoil Christmas Day festivities for my friends, but they knew my loss. I had married my friend Norton two months before, and our close friend Edith mourned with him for me.

"I'm so glad it didn't happen before you were married," she said to him. "You can more or less take Pat's place."

"Yes," said Norton gravely. "I just hope nothing happens to Dora."

When Dora is gone, God rest her wicked soul, and if Chrissie fails me, I think I shall not make or eat ice cream again, for there is no substitute for perfection. Probably Dora's best ice creams are her mango, peach and strawberry. Here the sweet massive cream blends with the subtle flavor of the fruit to make an ice cream so superlative that one becomes faint with ecstasy —or indigestion.

Mango Ice Cream

> 3 cups sieved mangos
> 1 cup chilled boiled custard
> ¾ cup sugar
> Juice of 1 to 1½ lemons
> 2 cups Dora's cream

Peel the mangos and put through a sieve. It takes about four large Haden mangos to make three cups of pulp. Stir in the sugar and the lemon juice. Blend with the custard. Stir in well the heavy cream. Taste for sweetness and acidity, adding more sugar or lemon juice to taste, remembering that cream will be less sweet after freezing. Freeze in a hand-freezer, using three parts ice to one part salt. Drain off salt water, remove dasher, licking, and repack with fresh ice and salt. Let stand one to two hours before serving, to mellow. When hurried, I have made this and other ice creams with three cups of Dora's cream, eliminating the custard, but I find that the custard gives a desirable body and texture to the ice cream.

Mango Ice Cream au Rhum

Peel and slice in three-eighths-inch thick slices, fresh ripe mangos. One mango will make the side dressing for four servings. Place in a shallow dish such as a soup plate and sprinkle with one-quarter cup powdered sugar to every mango, and one-third cup rum. Let stand in ice box one hour. Serve ice cream in glasses and arrange mango slices around each serving, pouring on a little of the liquid. This is the last word in desserts.

Strawberry Ice Cream

2½ cups strained strawberry juice
    (2 qt. boxes)
1 cup sugar
Juice 1½ to 2 lemons
1 cup chilled boiled custard
2 cups Dora's cream

Blend in order. Amount of sugar and of lemon juice depends on tartness of strawberries. Strawberry ice cream lends itself the best of any ice creams to an exclusive use of Dora's cream, and I am likely to use three cups of cream and no custard. Freeze and repack.

Fresh Peach Ice Cream

Use the same proportions as for strawberry ice cream, using two and one-half cups of peaches after peeling and putting through a sieve. More lemon juice is likely to be needed than for strawberry ice cream.

Rum and Coffee Ice Cream

2 cups hot boiled custard
1 cup steel-cut coffee
1½ cups cold water
Pinch of salt
2 cups Dora's cream
½ cup sugar
2 teaspoons vanilla
6 tablespoons rum

Make an infusion of the coffee and cold water by simmering three minutes. Strain into the hot custard. Cool and chill in ice box. When ready to freeze, add the cream, sugar, and salt and blend well. Stir in the vanilla and rum and freeze.

Ginger Ice Cream

2 cups chilled boiled custard
4 cups Dora's cream
1 tablespoon vanilla
Pinch of salt
½ cup Canton ginger
3 tablespoons ginger syrup
2 tablespoons sherry

Blend the chilled custard and the cream, stir in vanilla and salt. Add the ginger minced very fine, the ginger syrup, and the sherry. Freeze.

Peppermint Ice Cream

1 cup boiled custard, made with half
    the usual quantity of sugar
10 penny peppermint sticks
1 cup rich milk
2 cups Dora's cream

Crush the peppermint sticks and place with the milk over boiling water. Stir occasionally until candy is entirely dissolved. Blend with the custard and chill. Add cream and freeze. This is a lovely pale pink and has just the right peppermint flavor.

Orange Ice Cream

2 cups medium heavy cream
2 cups orange juice
Sugar to taste, about ½ cup

Stir cream very slowly into orange juice, sweeten and freeze. If oranges are at all insipid, add one tablespoon lemon juice. A little grated orange rind is also a pleasant addition.

Grape Juice Ice Cream

1 pt. bottled grape juice
½ to 1 cup sugar (to taste)
Juice of 1 lemon
3 cups medium heavy cream

Blend and freeze. This has an unusual flavor, pleasantly tart. By making with thin cream, or even rich milk, a more sherbet like cream results, suitable for use after a heavy dinner.

Canton Sherbet

4 cups water
1 cup sugar
¼ lb. Canton ginger
½ cup orange juice
⅓ cup lemon juice

Cut ginger in very small pieces, add to water and sugar and boil fifteen minutes. Add fruit juice and cool. The ginger may be strained out if preferred. Freeze. This is also delicious served as an accompaniment to certain meats, particularly wild duck, venison or country ham.

Orange Sherbet

I seldom make orange sherbet, as through the winter, when the oranges are in season, tangerines are, too, and tangerine sherbet has a decided edge on orange sherbet. In late spring, strawberries are in, followed by peaches and then mangos, and these ice creams are preferred. But at odd times I am grateful for the oranges handy on the trees, and make sherbet of them.

> 1 cup sugar
> 1 cup water
> 2 cups orange juice
> Juice of 1 or 2 lemons
> Grated rind of 2 oranges

Boil sugar and water ten minutes. Add grated rind, cool slightly, then add fruit juices. Chill, strain and freeze. Amount of sugar and lemon juice varies according to the acidity of the oranges.

Tangerine Sherbet

This is a Cross Creek *spécialité du maison*. Friends cry for it
It is to my winter what mango ice cream is to the summer. I
has an extremely exotic flavor and is a gorgeous color. Actually
it is very simple, and the only tricks to it are in having one'
own tangerine trees—and the patience to squeeze the juice from
at least a twelve-quart water bucket of the tangerines. In the
days when black 'Geechee lived with me, it was always he
choice for desserts, knowing its popularity. We usually had
crowd and served buffet, and 'Geechee would race through the
farmhouse, cap awry, bearing a loaded tray, and shouting at the
top of her strong lungs, "Tangerine sherbet comin' up! Sherbe
comin' up!"

1 cup sugar
1½ cups water
Juice of 1 or 2 lemons
4 cups tangerine juice
Grated rind of 4 tangerine

Boil sugar and water ten min
utes. Add the grated tangerin
rind to syrup while hot. Let coo
slightly and add tangerine juic
and lemon juice. Taste fo
sweetness and acidity, as th
tangerines vary. Chill thor
oughly, strain, and freeze.

Preserves, Jellies and Marmalades

I am giving only a few of such recipes that I myself use most frequently at Cross Creek. If any reader is seriously interested in a comprehensive list of Florida jellies, preserves and marmalades, there is no better compilation anywhere than in a bulletin issued by the Home Demonstration Division of the State of Florida Department of Agriculture, Tallahassee, Florida. In 1922, whence my copy dates, it was Bulletin No. 42. The same department issues, at a slight cost, or did issue, two other very valuable pamphlets: Florida Fruits and Vegetables in the Family Menu (Bulletin No. 46) and Florida Fruits and Vegetables in the Commercial Menu. I cannot give the number of the latter bulletin, as the Cross Creek cockroaches have eaten it off. (I do keep a clean house, but the cockroaches are wild wood roaches and come in with the wood that we use for the fireplaces and the old-fashioned wood stove.)

Scotch Marmalade

For years I struggled to make marmalade that would approximate the Scotch or best English orange marmalade—slightly bitter, tangy and clear. It seemed absurd to be raising oranges for a living, in the heart of the citrus belt, and not be able to make the perfect marmalade. I used ordinary oranges and the marmalade was too sweet. I used wild, or sour, oranges, which we raise as a root stock for the grafting of the sweet oranges, and it was only sour, without the *something* of Scotch and English marmalade. Then an old man who lived across Orange Lake from me said, "I suppose you know you have a tree of the true Seville orange on your place? My father gave the seed to an owner of your property."

All was suddenly clear. Of course, the English and Scotch imported Seville oranges from Spain for their manufacture of marmalade. But where was my tree? I questioned old colored Martha, who had worked on my place fifty years ago. She was demure, but at last truthful.

"Why, sugar," she said, "I thought you knowed. It's that tree just across the ditch, by the big palm tree, in the east grove. Nobody never picked the oranges, and I figgered you wasn't payin' them no mind, and I been usin' them to make marmalade. I calls them the bitter-sweet."

Martha and I went together across the drainage ditch, by the big palm tree in the east grove, and there stood a spindling tree covered with oranges that I had assumed to be only the wild or sour oranges. Now I saw the difference. They were not as rough and knobby as the wild oranges. I picked a few—and had my Scotch marmalade. The same method of preparation may be used for wild, or sour orange marmalade, which has its points, and has a liveliness lacking in sweet orange marmalade.

Wash fruit, remove peel, discarding two-thirds of the peel, retaining the third most free from blemishes. Cut this peel in as thin strips as possible. Place in a kettle and add water four times in weight to that of peel. Boil ten minutes, then drain. Repeat this process three times, each time bringing the water to a boil and boiling for five minutes. Cook until peel is extremely tender.

Weigh the fruit of the oranges, cut in small pieces, and for every pound of fruit add one quart of cold water. Boil until it is thoroughly disintegrated. Strain through a jelly bag, pressing well, then strain again through a flannel jelly bag without pressing.

Mix juice and peel, and to every pound of the mixture add one and one-half pounds of sugar. Boil rapidly together until the jellying point is reached, when the mixture will flake or sheet from the spoon. Turn into glasses or jars and seal.

Grapefruit Marmalade

Follow recipe for Scotch marmalade, using only one pound of sugar instead of one and one-half pounds to every pound of mixture.

Combination Marmalade

1 orange
1 grapefruit
1 lemon

This is quick and easy and very satisfactory, but does not have the exquisite transparency of the other recipe. Wash the fruit, remove seeds, and put it through a food chopper. Add three times the bulk of water, boil for fifteen minutes, and let stand overnight. Boil for ten minutes and let stand until cold. To every two cups of fruit add two cups of sugar. Boil rapidly until jellying stage is reached. With a cooking thermometer, this is two hundred and twenty-two degrees Fahrenheit.

Kumquat Marmalade

1 lb. kumquats
1 lb. sugar
1 qt. water

Boil one-fourth of kumquats one minute in water to cover. Drain. Cut the fruit horizontally in halves. Press out the pulp and save to add to the remaining whole kumquats. Cut the skins of this quarter-portion in very thin strips. Boil until tender, drain and set aside for adding to the jelly. Sprinkle the whole kumquats with one tablespoon soda. Cover with boiling water and let stand ten minutes. Drain and rinse three times in cold water. Put kumquats and quart of cold water in kettle and boil for thirty minutes. Strain through cheesecloth, pressing well. Then strain the juice through a flannel bag without pressing. Place the juice and the cooked strips of kumquat rind together in a kettle and bring to a boil. Add the pound of sugar slowly. Stir well. Let boil until it reaches the jellying point, two hundred and twenty-two degrees Fahrenheit, or when the jelly flakes or sheets from the spoon.

Kumquat Jelly

Make as for kumquat marmalade, but do not add any extra rind to the clear jelly.

Mayhaw Jelly

> 1 lb. mayhaws (ripe, but
>   not soft)
> 1 lb. sugar
> 1 qt. water

Wash mayhaws and boil with the water until tender, about twenty minutes. Strain through a jelly bag. Place juice in a kettle, bring to a boil, add sugar slowly, stirring. Let boil until jellying point is reached. I first had this delicate rosy-pink jelly on a bear hunt near the St. John's River. A big burly Cracker six feet tall had brought it along, of his wife's making, as his contribution to our food on the hunt.

Roselle Jelly

The roselle is usually called the Florida cranberry. It seems to be a member of the cotton ond okra families, as the decorative flowers resemble the flowers of those plants. The fleshy calyces only are used, after the blooms have formed pods that resemble rose hips.

Remove the calyces from the seed pods and for each measure of fruit allow two measures of water. Boil ten minutes, cover the kettle and let cool. Strain through a flannel jelly bag. To each cup of Roselle juice, add one-quarter cup orange pectin. This is made by mixing one-quarter pound of the white portion of orange peel, ground fine, with two tablespoons lemon juice and one cup cold water. Let stand four or five hours. Add two and one-half cups cold water and let stand overnight. Boil ten minutes, cool thoroughly, and strain through a flannel jelly bag, pressing well.

To each cup of mixed Roselle juice and orange pectin, brought to a boil, add one cup sugar slowly, stirring. Boil to the jellying point.

Mango Chutney

1 lb. peeled sliced mangos, not too ripe
2 cups vinegar or
1 cup grapefruit juice and 1 cup vinegar
½ lb. currants
½ lb. raisins (or use all raisins)
¼ lb. blanched almonds
3 oz. sliced green ginger or
3 oz. dried root ginger broken fine, put in spice bag and later removed
¾ lb. brown sugar
1 tablespoon salt
½ tablespoon white mustard seed (may go in spice bag with root ginger for later removal)
½ cup chopped onions
½ cup chopped sweet peppers
1 oz. chillies or hot peppers

Bring sugar and vinegar to a boil. Add spices and other ingredients, bring to a boil and boil thirty minutes.

Loquat Chutney

Substitute peeled and seeded loquats for mangos.

Guava Jelly

I use the very tart Cattley guavas. Ordinary guavas require the addition of some citric acid. Wash guavas, remove blossom end, slice thin. To every pound of guavas add one quart cold water and boil until very soft, about thirty minutes. Cool. Strain through cheesecloth, pressing, then through flannel without pressing. Bring juice to a boil and to every cup of juice add one cup sugar slowly, stirring. Boil until jellying point is reached.

Passion Fruit Jelly

Wash and slice about five quarts of fully ripe passion fruit. Add one and one-half cups cold water and simmer for fifteen minutes, mashing twice with a wooden masher. Strain through cheesecloth, pressing well, then through flannel or double cheesecloth, without pressing.

To every four cups of juice add six and one-half cups sugar, bring rapidly to boiling, and boil one minute. Add one-half cup liquid commercial pectin and remove from fire, stir well, skim quickly and turn at once into hot sterilized glasses, sealing while hot with melted paraffin.

Wild Grape, Wild Plum, Wild Blackberry Jelly

Mash fruit with wooden masher, without crushing seeds, barely cover with water and boil until fruit is disintegrated. Strain through cheesecloth, pressing, then through flannel without pressing. Bring juice to a boil, and to every cup of juice add one cup sugar slowly, stirring. Boil rapidly until jellying point is reached.

Loquat Preserves

1 lb. loquats
¾ lb. sugar
1½ cups water

Wash, scald, peel and seed loquats. Bring sugar and water to a boil, add loquats, and cook until tender and transparent.

"Better a Dinner of Herbs"

A friend said recently, "You and Idella are both such good cooks, you must feast when you're alone." I was peculiarly taken aback, for Idella and I alone are likely to eat food that is definitely "scrappy." The ingredients are at hand, Dora's cream and butter fill the ice box, ducks and frying chickens range over the grove, the pantry is filled with canned mushrooms, artichokes, crab and lobster meat, and so forth. Yet a poached egg, or a sandwich, or a bowl of warmed-over vegetables, and a glass of milk, are usually all that occurs to me for supper, while Idella wanders back to the tenant house with a bit of bread and bacon.

216

It never occurs to me to turn out an elaborate meal without "company" to partake.

For that reason, any sin of richness or expense in many of these recipes must be laid to the fact that they are "company" dishes. Yet among them are the cheap and simple things, the Hopping John, the white bacon with creamed potatoes, the practically costless fried cooter or gopher stew. And I recall the numbers of times friends have begged to come out just for collard greens, cornbread and Dora's buttermilk. We have just as good a time with this menu, and it tastes as good, as the ham baked in sherry, with orange baskets.

Two elements enter into successful and happy gatherings at table. The food, whether simple or elaborate, must be carefully prepared; willingly prepared; imaginatively prepared. And the guests—friends, family or strangers—must be conscious of their welcome. Formal dinners of ill-assorted folk invited for the sole purpose of repaying social obligations, are an abomination. The breaking together of bread, the sharing of salt, is too ancient a symbol of friendliness to be profaned. At the moment of dining, the assembled group stands for a little while as a safe unit, under a safe roof, against the perils and enmities of the world. The group will break up and scatter, later. For this short time, let them eat, drink and be merry.

Guests are acutely conscious of the spirit in which they have been invited, of the thoughts of the hostess while the meal has been planned and prepared. The suavest of manners, the most dazzling of table appointments, cannot hide the "duty" function. The magnificently moulded mousse, the crêpes suzettes, are tasteless. The mother or wife who grumbles over the planning and cooking of meals, taints the very vitamins. On the other hand, I have sat down to many a meal of grits and bacon and cornpone in backwoods cabins, that tasted utterly delicious because of the hearty pleasure of host and hostess in having company share their fare. No greater offense can be given in the rural South than to refuse a meal. Some slight apology may be made for the leanness.

"Reckon 'tain't what you're used to, but the greens is bound to be nice, for they're fresh picked." Or, " 'Tain't much, but it's the best we got, and you're sure welcome."

Such an apology is not in the class with that of the hostess who laments publicly, with embarrassment to the guests, that the ice cream is not firm, or the meat properly cooked, or the service is slow. She gives herself away as being more concerned with her own pride than the comfort of her guests. And the hostess who *twitters* might just as well announce that the company is unwanted.

So, I recommend Mother's war-time eggless cake as earnestly as her almond cake; cheap fried fish and hush-puppies as sincerely as baked whole chicken; pokeweed on toast as lustily as Dora's crab Newburg. The delight of friends and family in being together is the thing.

"Better a dinner of herbs where love is."

Index

Index

Printed in the United States
By Bookmasters